C000127733

Dr Richard Shumack lives in Sydne
of religion specializing in Muslim
Director of the Arthur Jeffery Ce
Melbourne School of Theology, t
RZIM Understanding and Answ
research fellow at the Centre for Public Christianity (CPX), Sydney,
Australia. Richard has published many articles in the Australian
media.

'I strongly recommend *Jesus through Muslim Eyes*: if you care about Muslim-Christian relations, this book is significant.'
Dr Muhammad Kamal, Asia Institute, University of Melbourne

'This is a profound book, written with deceptive simplicity and charm, like your previous book on Christianity's encounter with Islam. Its conclusions are fair-minded, provocative – and devastating for any who think simplistically about the Jesus Christ of Christian faith and the Isa ibn Maryam of the Qu'ran.'
Dr Shabbir Akhtar, Faculty of Theology, University of Oxford

'In this excellent book, Richard Shumack strikes the perfect balance between academic rigour and accessibility. Its discussion of the Islamic Jesus is lucid, and its application to the needs of Christian readers is highly relevant.'
Professor Peter Riddell, Professorial Research Associate, SOAS University of London

'Richard Shumack's familiarity with Islam gives him the ability to present a true picture of the religion in a way that is not unfair or uncharitable. Rather, he describes for us an accurate picture of how Islam sees and presents Jesus and compares that picture with the Jesus of history. Shumack has a knack for raising interesting questions and thoughtful arguments while expressing them in easy to understand ways. In *Jesus Through Muslim Eyes* he does just that.'
Abdu Murray, author of *Saving Truth: Finding Meaning and Clarity in a Post-Truth World*

'This is an honest and scholarly analysis of the Muslim Jesus, the Christian Jesus, and the diverging paths Muslims and Christians chose to follow. It brings profound new insights into the historical, philosophical and textual discussions about Jesus. It is an excellent contribution to both contemporary Christian-Muslim dialogue and the historical Jesus.'
Anwar Mehammed, head of Islamic Studies at the Ethiopian Theological College, Addis Ababa

JESUS THROUGH MUSLIM EYES

Richard Shumack

First published in Great Britain in 2020

Society for Promoting Christian Knowledge
36 Causton Street
London SW1P 4ST
www.spck.org.uk

Copyright © Richard Shumack 2020

All rights reserved. No part of this book may be reproduced or transmitted in
any form or by any means, electronic or mechanical, including photocopying,
recording, or by any information storage and retrieval system, without permission
in writing from the publisher.

SPCK does not necessarily endorse the individual views contained in its
publications.

Scripture quotations are from the ESV Bible (The Holy Bible, English Standard
Version), copyright © 2001 by Crossway, a publishing ministry of Good News
Publishers. Used by permission. All rights reserved.

Qur'an version: *Translation of the Meaning of the Qur'an*, Saheeh International
Translation, Abdulqasim Publishing House: Riyadh, 1997.

British Library Cataloguing-in-Publication Data
A catalogue record for this book is available from the British Library

ISBN 978–0–281–08193–6
eBook ISBN 978–0–281–08194–3

1 3 5 7 9 10 8 6 4 2

Typeset by The Book Guild Ltd, Leicester
First printed in Great Britain by Ashford Colour Press

eBook by The Book Guild Ltd, Leicester

Produced on paper from sustainable forests

Special thanks to my new friend and editor Tony Collins (at SPCK) for believing in the project, and to my old friend and colleague Natasha Moore (at CPX) for continuing to teach me how to write properly. Without either of you this book would not have come to be.

Contents

Contents

Part 3
LOCATING JESUS

Part 4
FOLLOWING JESUS

A quick word about terms

Choosing words can be tricky in religious discussions. The same word can mean different things in different religions or be used variously within a religion. When the religions involved depend upon scriptures written in a number of ancient languages there is the added problem of translation. Despite these complexities, I have chosen in this non-scholarly book to, wherever possible, use the simplest English word available.

So, for example, in Islam the divine creator of the universe is called by the Arabic term 'Allah'. In Christianity and Judaism this creator's proper name is the Hebrew term 'Yahweh'. In English, the generic term for this creator is 'God'. Outside of direct quotes, then, I will simply speak of God. Similarly, I will speak of the English 'Jesus' and not the Muslim '*Isa*'.

One choice I've made is important to note. The word 'gospel' is both central to this discussion and used in various subtle ways in Christianity and Islam. I have adopted the following convention:

Gospel – the four biblical (canonical) biographies of Jesus.
gospel – any non-biblical biography of Jesus.
injeel – the biography of Jesus described by the Qur'an.
message of Jesus – the content of the 'gospel' (lit. good news).

A quick word about terms

Prologue: Meeting Jesus

Like many Australians of my generation, I first met the Christian Jesus as a little kid. He was the Jesus of church Sunday School and primary school Scripture classes. For me he was, mostly, the Jesus of Christmas nativity scenes and the Easter Bunny. In my imagination, his (Australianized) life began in a sheep trough in a bush shed, skipped across a few un-confronting and fun miracles – like walking on water – and landed at his resurrection because, you know, Easter Eggs! I remember hearing very little talk about things like him being a holy, divine Lord or him dying horribly on a cross. Instead, for me, his soundtrack was 'Carols by Candlelight'. There, the Jesus of 'Silent Night' was meek and mild. Whether through my disinterest, or the well-meaning design of my teachers, the biblical records of Jesus had been censored to create a 'G'-rated Jesus. If I had any interest in this Jesus at all, it was well gone by the time I became a teenager. Football, music, mucking about in the bush, and, of course, girls all appeared vastly more attractive and so there were far more important people to hang around with than him.

It was much later, at university, that I came to say that I had *properly* met the Christian Jesus. There, through reading the Bible on its own terms, I was confronted with the Jesus of the Gospels in all his rich complexity. In this 'grown-up' encounter (and much to my surprise) I discovered a Jesus whose supernatural origins carried profound worldview implications, whose miraculous acts were soaked in hitherto unrecognized layers of religious meaning, and whose extraordinary earthly end forced me to face the mysteries of my mortality. For me, at that crucial formative time of life, this Jesus offered me the best explanation of both the universe and my place in it. Perhaps more importantly, he also seemed to empower me to be a better person. The spiritual icing on the cake was that my philosophical and moral awakening was accompanied by a range of supernatural experiences – including a miraculous healing – that seemed to confirm that Jesus, was indeed, who he claimed to be: the resurrected, divine, Lord of my life. Obviously, this encounter forced me to abandon my earlier notions of Jesus. The 'Christmas and Easter' Jesus of my childhood was revealed as a superficial, childish myth. The biblical Jesus who replaced him was compelling, so I followed.

Much later again, however, I met yet *another* Jesus: the Muslim Jesus. My work had led me to be deeply connected to a Muslim community. Up to that point, like most Westerners, I had been ignorant of the beliefs of Islam. I certainly had little idea that they believed in Jesus. So, it came as another surprise when, a few years ago, I met my friend Abdi outside our local gym to find he was wearing a T-shirt that cried out in bold letters:

I LOVE JESUS
BECAUSE I AM A MUSLIM
AND HE WAS TOO!

Now, I was being told that Jesus was a Muslim. Wondering just what this meant, I remember asking Abdi just what he loved about Jesus. Was there anything this Muslim Jesus did, or said, that Abdi was drawn to? Sheepishly he answered, 'Actually, I don't know anything much about Jesus. It was just a free T-shirt from the mosque!' This was instructive. I quickly learnt that while virtually every Muslim I met believed Jesus to be a prophet of Islam, and claimed to be devoted to him, most knew almost nothing about him beyond three key things: he was miraculously born of a virgin, he was absolutely *not* divine, and he didn't die on a cross.

Over time, of course, I ended up having conversations with Muslims who knew the Islamic Jesus well. They showed me verses about him in the Qur'an, classical Muslim scholarship about him, and the traditional sayings attributed to Jesus. They also showed me historical and religious arguments outlining just why they believed

Christian beliefs about Jesus to be distorted. Soon I found myself in the situation where my Muslim friends were encouraging me to take yet another quantum step in my knowledge of Jesus. They were calling for another spiritual awakening: another turning away from an impoverished image of the Christian Jesus, and towards religious and philosophical maturity found in the Muslim Jesus.

What follows is my attempt to take my friends' challenge to consider the Muslim Jesus seriously. As far as is objectively possible for a committed Christian, in the following pages I seek to meet the Muslim Jesus, on his terms, and weigh up his claims to be the true Jesus of history and religion and worthy of my devotion.

Part 1

GETTING TO KNOW
THE MUSLIM JESUS

Looking back, it is no surprise that my friend Abdi knew so little of the Muslim Jesus. Despite being revered as one of Islam's greatest prophets, he is a difficult character to pin down. Like the fictional movie spy, Austin Powers, the Islamic Jesus is an 'international man of mystery' who flits across time and space, occasionally dropping in to perform extraordinary acts. To meet him properly, my plan is to walk chronologically through Islamic history and see where we bump into him.

After getting a feel for what Arabs already believed about Jesus before Islam emerged onto the scene, we will explore Jesus as he appears in the Muslim scripture (the Qur'an), Muslim historical traditions (the *hadith*, biographies and histories), as well as the later mystical devotional works dedicated to Jesus (the *Qisas al-Anbiya*). What we will see is that, even with a determined and systematic approach like this, the Muslim Jesus remains an enigmatic figure – both historically and religiously.

1

Jesus of Arabia

On a recent plane flight, I sat next to a young man who was covered in what looked like prison-style tattoos yet carried a full complement of Gucci luggage and accessories. I was wondering who he was when another woman on the flight asked him for his autograph for her daughter. Clearly, he was someone famous – and not the drug dealer I initially pinned him as!

Later I tried to describe him to my kids. Between my limited description and an internet search we were able to work out that he was Harry Styles, possibly the most famous pop singer in the world at the time, who was visiting Sydney for an awards show. Luckily for me, because Harry was so extraordinarily well known, only a cursory portrayal was required for people to know just who I was talking about, just where he fit in the scheme of things, and just why he was travelling to Australia. Something very similar was the case with Jesus when Islam arose in the Arab peninsula in the seventh century CE. He was so well known that even nomadic Bedouin had some sense of who he was!

Muhammad was not the first to introduce Jesus to the Arab people. Tarif Khalidi recognizes in his (excellent) book *The Muslim Jesus* that 'Islam was born in a time and place where the figure of Jesus was widely known'.[1] Saying this should not be controversial. Both secular history and Islamic tradition recognize that Islam did not arise in a religious vacuum and, despite the dominant religion in Arabia at the time of Muhammad being polytheism, it seems likely that most Arabs were acquainted with Judaism and Christianity. There existed thriving Jewish and Christian minorities throughout Arabia and so the Islamic traditions, including the Qur'an, find it entirely ordinary that Christians and Jews lived happily among the

Arabs. This is certainly the mainstream view of historical scholars. The great William Montgomery Watt points to the many points of contact between Arabs and Christians:

> The Byzantine empire, whose power and higher civilization they [the Arabs] greatly admired, was Christian, and so was Abyssinia. Even in the Persian empire Christianity was strong, and al-Hirah, the Persian vassal-state with which the Arabs were much in contact, was an outpost of the East Syrian or Nestorian Church. This combination of monotheism with military and political strength and a higher level of material civilization must have impressed the Arabs greatly. The nomadic tribes and settled communities in closest contact with these states were indeed being gradually Christianized; and even some of the Meccan merchants were not uninfluenced by what they saw when they traveled to the border market town on business. There were also Christians in Mecca, traders and slaves, but the influence of isolated individuals was probably not so important.

It wasn't only Christians. The Arabs were well acquainted with Jews and Judaism too:

> The opportunities for contact with Jews were not so extensive as those with Christians, but some were probably more intimate. This was especially so in Medina where Jews and pagan Arabs were settled side by side. There were also a number of Jewish tribes who settled at oases in Arabia and in the fertile parts of southern Arabia, either refugees of Hebrew race or Arab tribes which had adopted Judaism. There were apparently practically no Jews in Mecca.[2]

The Arabs, then, were well acquainted with Christian communities.
    Importantly, most of these large Christian communities held mainstream – orthodox – beliefs about Jesus. That is, they were Trinitarian and believed that Jesus was God. To be sure, some

non-mainstream groups and texts existed in the Arabian peninsula. Nevertheless, as Islam emerged, it overwhelmingly encountered followers of, and stories about, a divine Christian Jesus.

The idea that Islam's Jesus was presented in the shadow of a divine Jesus seems to make the most sense of the Muslim historical sources too. It is seen most clearly in the narrative of the visit to Muhammad of a delegation of Christians from Najran. Found in Ibn Ishaq's biography of the Prophet, this tradition makes crystal clear that the Najrani delegates held to the orthodox Trinitarian Christianity of the Byzantine empire. The narrator is also at great pains to emphasize that the party included a highly qualified Christian theologian, Abu Haritha, who possessed 'an excellent knowledge of their religion, and the Christian kings of Byzantium had honoured him and ... built churches for him'.[3] Here, then, we are dealing with at least some Christians with a high degree of religious sophistication. Naturally this led to some detailed debate between Muhammad and the delegates concerning the person of Jesus. Ibn Ishaq makes the pertinent observation that while all the party were Trinitarian there existed a range of positions on Jesus including: a) that he was God, b) that he was the Son of God, and c) that he was the Third person of the Trinity. Christians might be surprised to hear that these claims are incoherent, or necessarily represent different positions on Jesus – orthodox Christians like myself are happy to accept all three as true! For now, though, the key point is not the details of how these discussions progressed, but the mere fact that they happened at all. It shows that, while early Muslim historians clearly believed Trinitarian Christianity to be heretical, they also very likely believed it to be orthodox Christian belief in Arabia.

There are clues that it was not only Muhammad who was familiar with belief in a divine Jesus as the Christian norm. It seems his hearers were in the same position. It is well established that the Qur'anic text assumes its first hearers were familiar with various biblical characters and stories. So, the Qur'anic narratives concerning Moses, Noah, Imran, Mary – as well as Jesus – are not presented as new teaching but recounted as reminders of previous divine lessons.

A further clue is the call of the Qur'an for its hearers to seek confirmation of its message from the 'People of Remembrance' (*ahl al-dhikr*). So, Surah an-Nahl commends:

> And We sent not before you except me to whom we revealed. So ask the people of the message (ahl al-dhikr) if you don't know. (Q16.43)

Commentators have debated the precise meaning of this *ahl al-dhikr* term. However, it is common to take it to mean Christians (and perhaps Jews). This fits the context in Surah 16. Here we have a call to compare the message of the Qur'an with that of previous revelations, i.e. the Torah and *Injeel* (gospel). For this suggestion to make any sense at all it requires the hearers of the Qur'an to have easy access to these people or stories or texts. Obviously, this requires them to know either Christians, or the Bible.

Yet more clues to Muhammad's partly Christian context exist in the Qur'an in the form of challenges concerning the source of his recitations. It appears that Muhammad's opponents were accusing him of depending upon earthly sources for his recitations. So, in Surah al-Furqan we find:

> And those who disbelieve say, 'This Qur'an is not except a falsehood he invented, and another people assisted him in it.' But they have committed an injustice and a lie. And they say, 'Legends of the former peoples which he has written down, and they are dictated to him morning and afternoon.' (Q 25.4–5)

And, again, in Surah an-Nahl we read:

> And We certainly know that they say, 'It is only a human being who teaches him…' (Q16.103)

Whatever the substance behind these allegations, the very fact they are being made at all likely points to the existence of people in Muhammad's society who are well known for narrating these 'legends of the former peoples.' Again, this points most obviously to the Christians and the Jews.

Before Islam, then, the Jesus of Arabia was essentially the orthodox Christian Jesus. The Arabs knew orthodox Christians, knew stories about Jesus, knew people who narrated these stories, knew these stories were grounded in scriptures, knew various doctrines about Jesus, and some even knew details of Christian debates over how their Messiah could be both human and divine. Of course, the prophet of Islamic monotheism was not comfortable with these Trinitarian elements in the image of Jesus, so as Muhammad began his prophetic ministry he set about proclaiming what he saw as the true account of Jesus and what it was proper to believe about him. It is this Qur'anic Jesus we need to meet next.

2

The son of Mary:
the Qur'anic Jesus

The Qur'an doesn't go out of its way to introduce us to Jesus. Nor does it outline a comprehensive biography of his life. Instead, as we've just seen, it appears to simply assume we know who it is talking about. Still, we run into him strikingly often, and it is immediately obvious that he is a singular figure. The intriguing details we are given shows he stands alone among the prophets of Islam.

Jesus' Qur'anic biography is extraordinary. The key features the Qur'an is interested in are highlighted in this verse in Surah al-Ma'ida (The Table):

> O Jesus, Son of Mary, remember My favor upon you and upon your mother when I supported you with the Pure Spirit and you spoke to the people in the cradle and in maturity; and when I taught you writing and wisdom and the Torah and the Gospel; and when you designed from clay like the form of a bird with My permission, then you breathed into it, and it became a bird with My permission; and you healed the blind and the leper with My permission; and when you brought forth the dead with my Permission; and when I restrained the Children of Israel from you when you came to them with clear proofs and those who disbelieved among them said, 'This is not but obvious magic'. (Q5.110)

This text mirrors the Qur'an as a whole by putting special emphasis on: Jesus' miraculous birth and the events leading up to it; the idea that Jesus taught a gospel; the miracles performed by Jesus to confirm his prophethood; and God's rescue of Jesus from the persecution of the Jews by taking him directly to heaven (thereby avoiding the crucifixion). No other Qur'anic prophet displays anything like this life trajectory.

These striking biographical highlights hint that there is something religiously special about Jesus too. Most famously Surah an-Nisa spells out that:

> The Messiah, Jesus, the son of Mary, was but a messenger of Allah and His word which he directed to Mary and a soul from Him. So believe in Allah and his messengers. And do not say 'Three'; desist it is better for you. Indeed Allah is but one God. Exalted is he above having a son. To Him belongs whatever is in the heavens and whatever is on the earth. (Q 4.171)

The interesting thing here is not that the Qur'an denies the divinity of Jesus. That claim follows naturally from (arguably) the main theme of the Qur'an: the absolute oneness and supremacy of God. No, the *really* interesting thing here is that Jesus is ascribed three extraordinary and unique theological qualities: 1) the role of Messiah, 2) the identity as a word from God, and 3) another identity as a soul, or spirit, from God.

Now frustratingly for us perhaps, the Qur'an offers very little explanation on either Jesus' outstanding biographical features or his religious importance. Certainly, in comparison to the rich character we meet in the Christian Gospels, the Qur'anic Jesus remains a deeply mysterious fellow. We are told virtually nothing of his teaching, or his movements or his ministry patterns, or his character, or his interactions with ordinary people. Indeed, we know far more about his mother and grandparents than him!

We also hear virtually nothing of Jesus' prophetic voice. Khalidi describes the Qur'an recording conversations between Jesus and either God or the Israelites.[4] However, it is more accurate to describe the Qur'an recording references to, or summaries of, such conversations. So, Jesus is occasionally heard making some general declarations like: 'I am just a messenger' (Q61.6) or 'Allah is my Lord and your Lord' (Q43.64) or 'O Children of Israel worship Allah my Lord…' (Q5.72). Again, though, these remain fleeting and seem aimed at deflecting attention away from himself.

Just once we hear him in prayer:

> O Allah, our Lord, send down to us a table from heaven to be for us a festival for the first of us and the last of us and a sign from You. And provide for us, and You are the best of providers. (Q5.114)

Notice the character of this prayer: it is brief, general, and corporate. It bears little resemblance to the intensely detailed and personal prayers we see Jesus praying in the Gospels.

Similarly, the Qur'an leaves us wondering just what it has in mind concerning Jesus' titles. So, we can ask questions like: Just what is a Messiah in Islam and does the role have any religious significance? Just how is Jesus a word from God? Is this true of other prophets too? If not, why is it singled out here? In short, the seeker for the Muslim Jesus is easily left wondering why the Qur'an gives us so little insight into Jesus the person. Why the mystery?

The first, and most obvious answer to this question is this: Jesus is simply not the key focus of the Qur'an. He is merely an incidental character. When we consider the main themes of the Qur'an this answer makes sense. The Qur'an is primarily interested in three main ideas:

1. The oneness and supremacy of God.
2. The divine nature of the Qur'anic recitation (and therefore Muhammad's prophetic credentials).
3. The warning of coming judgement.

Usually, when earlier prophets are referred to, they are merely called in as witnesses confirming that the Qur'an stands in a long line of divine messages. Only as much of their backstories are brought in as is necessary to establish their *bona fides* as witnesses. Similarly, only as much of their teaching is referenced as is necessary to confirm that they were Islamic monotheists. Along this line of thinking, the Qur'an's interest in Jesus is mainly that – like Muhammad – he was merely a prophet and that – like Muhammad – he simply taught Islam. Enough said. Taken on its own terms, this seems a sensible response.

A second, also sensible, explanation for the lack of detail is that when the Qur'an does focus its attention on Jesus it is for the purposes of correction of error. Khalidi points out that 'the Qur'anic Jesus, unlike any other prophet, is embroiled in polemic'.[5] This is because, uniquely among the prior prophets, the Qur'an sees the need to 'cleanse' Jesus from the supposedly false doctrines he accumulated around him. This purifying role is made clear is Surah al-Maryam:

> When Allah said, 'O Jesus, indeed I will take you and raise you to Myself and purify you from those who disbelieve and make those who follow you superior to those who disbelieve until the Day of Resurrection. Then to Me is your return, and I will judge between you concerning that which you used to differ.' (Q3.55)

And, straightforwardly, the doctrines the Qur'an is at greatest pains to purify Jesus from are those claiming his divinity. So, we find in Surah al-Ma'idah (the Table):

> And when Allah will say, 'O Jesus, Son of Mary, did you say to the people, 'Take me and my mother as deities besides Allah?' He will say, 'Exalted are You! It was not for me to say that to which I have no right. If I had said it, You would have known it. You know what is within myself, and I do not know what is within Yourself. Indeed, it is You who is Knower of the unseen.' (Q5.116)

This makes sense too. The Qur'an's passionate concern to champion the uniqueness and oneness of Allah naturally leads to its similarly passionate concern to ruthlessly dismiss any doctrine that challenges this. The Qur'an, then, is all about Allah and so when it comes to Jesus the Qur'an is merely interested in confirming Jesus' own focus on Allah, and correcting his followers' distorted beliefs.

This all makes sense – to a point. Jesus may not be a key character. He may well be the victim of erroneous claims. But this doesn't remove the enigma that surrounds what the Qur'an *does* say about him. For every verse affirming how ordinary he is as a prophet, there is another highlighting his extraordinariness. For every negative correction of a supposedly false Christian doctrine of Christ, there is a positive allusion to a mysterious Islamic doctrine of Christ. At first glance then, Jesus, the Son of Mary, who we meet in the Qur'an, remains perplexing. He appears too biographically and religiously 'thin' to fully explain himself. Happily, though, other Muslim traditions worked to put some flesh on these prophetic bones.

3

The 'pious servant': the traditional Jesus

The sovereign of Australia – the Queen of England – is hard to get to know personally. As head of a constitutional monarchy, she properly keeps things formal and her private opinions to herself. Nevertheless, I have come to know some intimate personal details about her character, her family, and even her spiritual life. This is because one of my close friends grew up at Sandringham Palace, the Queen's private residence. Indeed, her father was one of the Queen's chaplains and so the royal family used to regularly drop by for morning tea after chapel. Over time they became close. Fortunately for us, there is a similar potential to get to know the Muslim Jesus in more detail than is provided in the Qur'an. Muslim tradition records a number of personal interactions with Jesus, beginning with Muhammad's own encounters.

The *hadith*

We meet Jesus again in the *hadith* tradition – that is, the recorded sayings and actions of the prophet Muhammad. There the Qur'anic Christ is fleshed out in more detail – literally! So, we find reports of Muhammad meeting Jesus (in heaven) and describing his physical appearance. For example:

The Prophet said, 'I saw Moses, Jesus and Abraham (on the night of my Ascension to the heavens). Jesus was of red complexion, curly hair and a broad chest. Moses was of brown complexion, straight hair and tall stature as if he was from the people of Az-Zutt'.[6]

Elsewhere Muhammad describes Jesus as being: of medium height; well built; crisp-haired; lank-haired; red-faced 'as if he had come out of a bathroom'; and, interestingly, resembling someone named Urwa b. Mas'ud![7] The significance of these descriptions of Jesus, though debated, remains cryptic. Perhaps all we can say with confidence is that Jesus changes his hair style regularly!

Of course, we might hope the *hadith* would add some religious substance to the Muslim Jesus. For the most part, unfortunately, they don't. In the mainstream Sunni hadith, we meet substantially the same Jesus we met in the Qur'an. Muhammad is at pains to emphasize that despite being called the Word and Spirit of God, Jesus remains (over and over) merely a 'pious servant'. Along these lines much is made in the hadith of Jesus' inability to intercede with God on behalf of people and his similar prophetic status to Muhammad.

There is, however, one area where the *hadith* provide fresh insight. It concerns Jesus' role in the judgement day. Despite a virtual silence in the Qur'an concerning the role of the Messiah, we discover in the hadith that the Messiah plays a dominant role at the end of the present age. Here is perhaps the most detailed description:

> ... and it will be at this very time that Allah will send 'Isa [Jesus], son of Maryam [Mary] who will descend at the white minaret in the eastern side of Damascus, wearing two garments lightly dyed and placing his hands on the wings of two angels. When he will lower his head, there would fall drops of water from his head, and when he will raise it up, drops like pearls would scatter from it. Every disbeliever who will find his (i.e., 'Isa's) smell will die and his smell will reach as far as he will be able to see. He will then search for Dajjal until he will catch hold of him at the gate of Ludd (village near Jerusalem), and will kill him. Then the people, whom Allah will have protected, will come to 'Isa son of Maryam, and he will wipe their faces and will inform them of their ranks in Jannah...[8]

Again, we see just how extraordinary the Muslim Jesus is! He is given responsibility for executing judgement on all unbelievers, destroying the anti-Christ (*Al-Masih Ad-Dajjal*), and then welcoming the believers into heaven. Wow!

Yet again this gives rise to questions. One that jumps out immediately is: Just who is the Dajjal, or the anti-Christ? He is an even more mysterious being than the Muslim Jesus. The brief description of him in the hadith is of a one-eyed counterfeit Jesus seeking to deceive humans into following false religion. We are told nothing of what type of being he is – is he human or supernatural? – or where he fits in the pantheon of deceiving spirits in Islam. Whoever the Dajjal is, his very existence serves to highlight the honoured role Jesus plays in the Muslim judgement day: the Muslim Christ is significant enough to warrant an anti-hero!

Here's another question: Why, in Islam, is Jesus the one given these key roles at judgement day? Of course, God is free to use whoever he chooses as an agent of judgement or salvation. Still, it is striking that, given Jesus is simply an ordinary prophet, he is the one given the job. Why not Muhammad? Or Gabriel? And again, we are given no explanation. If the Qur'anic Jesus is enigmatic, then instead of bringing the Muslim Jesus into clearer focus as a mere prophet of Islam, the hadith add to his enigma.

The *Sira*

Unfortunately, our quest to get to know the Muslim Jesus better is not aided greatly when we turn to Ibn Ishaq's biography of Muhammad – the *Sira*. We find passing reference to him by Muhammad in a variety of contexts, but most times these sayings merely confirm the Qur'an's teaching. So, again, Jesus is: the son of Mary; virgin born; of flesh and blood and hair and skin (like David); the Spirit and Word of God; the cousin of John; had disciples; taught and confirmed the Torah and the gospel; raised the dead; created birds; healed the sick; and was raised to God.

There is, however, one report where we learn a new and interesting thing about Jesus' life and ministry. In an account of Muhammad sending messengers to various kingdoms inviting them to embrace Islam we see him warning his hearers not to 'hang back from me as the disciples held back from Jesus.' This story involves an incident where Jesus complained to God about his disciples refusing a long journey. The account continues:

> Those whom Jesus Son of Mary sent, both disciples and those who came after them, in the land were: Peter the disciple and Paul with him, (Paul belonged to the followers and was not a disciple) to Rome; Andrew and Matthew to the land of the cannibals; Thomas to the land of Babel which is the land of the East; Philip to Carthage which is Africa; John to Ephesus the city of the young men of the cave; James to Jerusalem which is Aelia the city of the sanctuary; Bartholomew to Arabia which is the land of the Hijaz; Simon to the land of the Berbers; Judah who was not one of the disciples was put in the place of Judas.[9]

Here, for the first time in the Muslim tradition, we find Jesus commissioning his followers to proclaim his message throughout the world. This is significant for at least three reasons.

First, it is significant just how closely this account of the early preaching of the gospel aligns with the traditional Christian account. As we will see in detail in later chapters, church tradition records the spread of the gospel message happening in just this way and with just these apostles travelling to just these places. Ibn Ishaq, the historian, finds no need to modify, or correct, this traditional story.

Second, it is significant that the apostle Bartholomew is recorded preaching in Arabia. This aligns with our earlier observation that the Arabs were familiar with the mainstream (i.e. Trinitarian) apostolic teaching about Jesus. As it happens, this also aligns with a minor tradition within Christianity that Bartholomew travelled east from Jerusalem, through Southern Arabia (today's Yemen), before ending up in India.

Third, this historical record is significant because it seems at odds with contemporary Muslim narratives concerning the distortion of Christianity by Jesus' followers. More on this soon.

Al-Tabari

The early Muslim historian who most fills out the narrative of the Qur'anic Jesus for us is the great al-Tabari. Indeed, he devotes close to two whole chapters of his magisterial history to Jesus, and the events surrounding his life. To his very great credit as an historian, al-Tabari often passes on competing – indeed sometimes conflicting – reports of events without seeking to harmonize them. We find him doing just this in providing extended, intricately detailed, yet slightly conflicting stories of Jesus' birth. As interesting as these nativity accounts are, though, they add little to us knowing the Muslim Jesus better. Two other historical reports, however, are far more interesting for our investigation.

The first report gives us subtle clues that the birth of the Messiah fulfils prophecy. So, al-Tabari is the first Muslim historian to properly set Jesus' ministry in its historical setting:

Some historians mentioned that Jesus was born forty-two years after Augustus had become emperor. Augustus continued to live on, and his reign lasted fifty-six years, some add a few days. The Jews assaulted Christ. The sovereign in Jerusalem at the time was Caesar, and it was on his behalf that Herod the Great reigned in Jerusalem. Messengers of the king of Persia came to him. Sent to Christ, they came to Herod by mistake. They informed Herod that the king of Persia had sent them to offer Christ the gifts they carried, gifts of gold, myrrh and frankincense. They told him that they had observed that Christ's star had risen – they had learned through computation. They offered him the gifts at Bethlehem in Palestine. When Herod learned about them, he plotted against Christ, and looked for him in order to slay him. God commanded an angel to tell Joseph, who was with

Mary at the sanctuary, that Herod intended to slay the child, and to instruct him to flee to Egypt with the child and its mother. When Herod died the angel told Joseph, who was in Egypt, that Herod was dead and that his son Archelaus reigned instead – the man who had sought to slay the child was no longer alive. Joseph took the child to Nazareth in Palestine, to fulfill the word of Isaiah the prophet, 'I called you out of Egypt.' Archelaus died, and the younger Herod became king, in whose reign the likeness of Christ was crucified.[10]

Al-Tabari generally does his best to cite his sources, but here we are left wondering just which 'historians' he is drawing his material from. In this case it seems likely that he is dependent upon Christian sources, with this report resonant with the Gospel of Matthew in virtually every detail – except one. Al-Tabari, or his sources, see fit to make one correction to Matthew: here the Muslim Jesus was not crucified. Instead it is only a 'likeness of Christ' that hung on a cross.

This correction is straightforwardly Islamic – but it doesn't remove all the problems from the report. There is another less obvious, but no less important, claim in this story. Just like in the Gospel of Matthew, Jesus' trip to Egypt while a child is viewed as a fulfilment of prophecy.[11] This should give us pause. It raises an intriguing question: How does Islam account for not just this, but all the prophecies about Jesus found in Old Testament?

We find a similar messianic conundrum in a second report (from al-Muthanna-Isliaq b. al-Hajjaj-Isma'il b. 'Abd al-Karim-'Abd al-Samad b. Ma'qil-Wahb):

What I have done with you tonight in serving you the meal, washing your hands with mine – this is to make you and me equal. You consider me the best of you, so do not be arrogant towards one another. Sacrifice yourselves for one another, just as I sacrifice myself for you. My request of you is that you call out to God; call out fervently to postpone my end.[12]

This is fascinating. Here (again!) we encounter Jesus' last supper with his disciples. This time we witness strong echoes of Jesus' words to his disciples in all four Christian Gospels. There, too, we read of Jesus humbling himself to serve, Jesus calling for his followers to be similarly humble, and Jesus asking his disciples to pray for him as he faces the end of his time on earth. All these are sensibly Islamic traits. One feature of the story, however, isn't: Jesus' call to sacrifice. Just what sort of sacrifice is this referring to?

Now, it is worth noting that as we have moved through the Muslim traditions, we have encountered decreasingly authoritative texts. So, the hadith carry more revelatory force than the Sira, and the Sira more than al-Tabari. (And the Sunni Hadith, the Sira and al-Tabari are likely to carry little force *at all* with Shia Muslims.) In light of this, I can imagine an argument that the sorts of Christological puzzles we have described are due to unreliability – particularly in the later texts. Perhaps. Nevertheless, these traditions remain the best available, and surely carry significant historical, if not divine revelatory, weight.

In any case, despite never straying far from his Qur'anic roots, the traditional Muslim Jesus remains, indeed grows, religiously paradoxical. Instead of the histories introducing us to the person behind the Qur'anic skeleton, they introduce us to new theological riddles to solve. As a result, he remains just as hard to know – and, consequently, no easier to love. Despite this, and perhaps because of it, there arose a parallel Jesus tradition in Islam. It flourished primarily in Sufism and this Sufi Jesus emerges as a radically different character. It's time to meet him.

4

The good teacher:
the Sufi Jesus

The perplexities and controversies surrounding Jesus, the Muslim Messiah, did not prevent many Muslims being attracted to Jesus as a model of Islamic asceticism (Sufism). Just where this Sufi Jesus emerged onto the scene from is unclear. What is clear, however, is that, once he had appeared, there developed an extraordinary corpus of traditions around him. There, for the first time, we are presented with rich details of the Muslim Jesus' teaching and his practice of the ordinary religious life.

Khalidi describes the arrival of this other Sufi Jesus into the Muslim imagination like this:

> Here, then, we see a parting of the ways. The Jesus of the eschaton was enshrined in authoritative Hadith collections, becoming a somewhat distant figure of no immediate or pragmatic moral relevance to Muslim piety. But another Jesus continued to prosper – the Jesus encountered in works of piety and asceticism and in a genre of religious literature called 'Tales of the Prophets' (Qisas al-Anbiya), where he was not only a living moral force but also a figure who played a role in intra-Muslim polemics. It is this other Jesus, the Jesus of popular piety and devotion, whose stories…continued to appear in the Arabic literature throughout the premodern period – that is, right up to the eighteenth century.[13]

The Sufi Jesus has one interesting thing in common with the Qur'anic Jesus. Just as Jesus stands out as extraordinary among the prophets referenced by the Qur'an, he also stands apart as unique among the prophets referenced by the *Qisas al-Anbiya*. Khalidi notes that:

> Whereas the sayings and tales of other prophets tend to conform to specific and narrowly defined moral types, the range and continuous growth of the Jesus corpus has no parallels among other prophets in the Muslim tradition.[14]

Indeed! This 'Jesus corpus' grew into a rich resource comprising literally hundreds of sayings. Some are short pithy proverbs like this one:

> Do not reward a wrongdoer with wrongdoing, for this will nullify your virtue in God's sight.[15]

Others are long narratives describing Jesus' interactions with fellow religious travelers. Perhaps the best way to meet this Sufi Jesus, is to follow his emergence via a brief overview of his teaching through the centuries.

So, we first meet him in the 8th century as a practical religious teacher who speaks with a tone reminiscent of the Qur'an:

> Do not talk much without the mention of God, lest your hearts grow hard; for the hard heart is far from God, but you do not know. Do not examine the sins of people as though you were lords, but examine them, rather, as though you were servants. Men are of two kinds; the sick and the healthy. Be merciful to the sick and give thanks to the healthy.[16]

By the ninth century, however, Jesus had adopted a distinctly Sufi lifestyle:

> Jesus was a constant traveler in the land, never abiding in a house or a village. His clothing consisted of a cloak made of coarse hair or camel stub and two hairless shirts. In his hand he carried a club. Whenever night fell, his lamp was the

moonlight, his shade the blackness of night, his bed the earth, his pillow a stone, his food the plants of the field. At times, he spent whole days and nights without food. In times of distress he was happy, and in times of ease he was sad.[17]

Truly I say to you, to eat wheat bread, to drink pure water, and sleep upon dunghills with the dogs more than suffices him who wishes to inherit paradise.[18]

Also, in the ninth century Jesus' sayings occasionally take on biblical notes. Witness this retelling of the Gospel of Matthew 6.21:

Place your treasures in heaven, for the heart of man is where his treasure is.[19]

By the tenth century he was commending an ascetic lifestyle in the strongest metaphorical terms:

Jesus would say to the world, 'Away from me, you pig!'[20]

The eleventh century Jesus continued the trend telling his followers to:

Leave yourselves to hunger and thirst, go naked and exhaust yourselves, that your hearts might know God Almighty.[21]

In the twelfth century Jesus' asceticism was championed by none other than the great al-Ghazali who recorded him claiming:

I have two loves – whoever loves them loves me, and whoever hates them hates me: poverty and pious exertion.[22]

Many of Jesus' early sayings bore echoes of the Gospels, but by the thirteenth century Muslim Jesus was sounding literally biblical. The following saying, recounted by the renowned Sufi Suhrawardi, not only virtually quotes the Gospel of John word for word, it also frames eternity using uniquely Christian concepts:

> He who has not been born twice shall not enter the Kingdom of Heaven.[23]

And this hadn't changed by the fifteenth century where Jesus said:

> O disciples, gold is a cause of joy in this world and a cause of harm in the afterlife. Truly I say to you, the rich shall not enter the Kingdom of Heaven.[24]

This Sufi Jesus we get to know through his *Qisas al-Abiya* sayings bears little resemblance to the Qur'anic/traditional Jesus. He has very little interest in polemics; lots of interest in piety. He is almost never the Messiah; almost always the simple teacher. He is deeply conscious of securing eternal life for his hearers; almost silent on the terrifying judgement day. He is profoundly God-focused, yet apparently uninterested in the formal rituals of Islam. In short, he is truly a mystic. Also, in contrast to the traditional Muslim Jesus, the Sufi Jesus is far more *knowable*. He is a real person, engaging with other real people concerning real life issues, yet seeking to point them heavenwards. He is inspiring in his simple, Godward, compassionate, serving, virtuous and virtuously wisdom sharing life.

Despite all this, however, the Sufi Jesus, too, remains a mystery man. For all the thousands of words we hear him speak, he is a man with no story. He has no place, no home, no family, no friends, no community, no origin, no purposeful journey and no destination. Poetically, yet problematically, the Sufi Jesus remains a figure untethered: he is unanchored in history, and religiously unformed.

Where, then, did the Sufi Jesus come from?

Khalidi suggests the answer to this question might be found in the clues provided by his developing character over time. So:

> First we have the ascetic saint; then comes the lord of nature, the miracle worker, the healer, the social and ethic model…

The Jesus of Islamic Sufism became a figure not easily distinguished from the Jesus of the Gospels, and one reason must undoubtedly have been the growing familiarity with the Gospels among Muslim scholars.[25]

Khalidi's explanation is that the Sufi Jesus arose out of the need to complement the thin Qur'anic account, and via religious 'seepage', i.e. 'intimate encounters with a living Christianity suffused with rich and diverse images of Jesus'.[26] This explanation seems obvious and sensible. The striking and unmistakable parallels between the sayings of the biblical Jesus and the Sufi Jesus are so close that borrowing from Christian tradition seems very likely.

Is this explanation controversial? Khalidi thinks it need not be. His idea is that any truth is valuable so long as it conforms to an Islamic framework:

> In this early period, the agenda of interaction between Islam and Christianity was not set solely by the Qur'an, but was also decided by the historical circumstances of social, spiritual, and indeed military encounter. What percolated from one community to the other was determined by what each saw as true or complementary or edifying in the traditions of the other, given the intimate spiritual affinities between them. For the early Muslims, there was no prima facie reason not to accept a Christian story, tradition, maxim, or homily, provided it lay within the conceptual framework that Islam had already laid out for itself.[27]

The crucial issue here, of course, is whether the teaching of the Sufi Jesus really does fit neatly into the 'conceptual framework' of traditional Islam. Does it? Generally, Jesus' simple Godward life appears eminently Islamic. Still, he often speaks using concepts alien to the Qur'an: like 'the Kingdom of Heaven', 'Kingdom of God', 'salvation', and speaking of God as 'Father'. Can these notions be properly Islamicized?

This is important. It will not do to have two Muslim Jesuses. If the traditional Muslim Messiah and the Sufi Jesus cannot be reconciled into one person then we will be faced with a difficult choice between a distant, enigmatic Messiah with a puzzling theological backstory, and an attractive and wise Mystic with no real spiritual home. Fortunately, recent work by Mustafa Akyol has provided at least one credible attempt to merge these parallel traditions into a single Muslim Jesus. Let's see who he came up with.

5

Yeshua: the contemporary Muslim Jesus

The premodern period of Islam introduced us to two Jesuses. There is the traditional Jesus, son of Mary, whom we meet in the most authoritative texts, who turned up for the purposes of apologetics, and who will turn up again for the purposes of judgement. Then there is Jesus the Sufi, who we meet in an eclectic sea of largely Christian oral traditions, and who turns up modelling the ideal ascetic religious life. Different Muslims have adopted one or the other of these Jesuses to suit their own purposes. Apologists coopted the traditional Jesus into their polemic encounters with Christianity, and straightforwardly he fit the role with aplomb. Mystics and interfaith religionists preferred the Sufi Jesus due to his rich piety and the obvious commonalities with the Jesus in Christian devotion.

As the character of the two Muslim Jesuses diverged over the years, there were few attempts to reconcile them into one coherent person – until now. In 2017 Mustafa Akyol presented us with *The Islamic Jesus: How the King of the Jews became a prophet of the Muslims*. Originally, intriguingly, and eloquently, he goes about introducing us to yet another Jesus – the Jesus of Jewish Christianity. In a nutshell his claim is this: it is not Islam that has two Jesuses, but Christianity. Drawing on controversial recent scholarship, Akyol's argument centres on the claim that very early on within Christianity there emerged a split between Jewish and Gentile traditions. Let's walk through his key points.

First, according to this theory, Jewish Christianity, based in Judea and led by James (the brother of Jesus), was original, strictly monotheistic and believed in a non-divine Jesus. An opposing tradition, Gentile Christianity, emerged later. It was centred in

Rome, led by Paul, and (heretically) developed the doctrines of the Trinity and a divine Jesus. Core to this theory is the idea that the Jesus of so-called Jewish Christianity was the true Jesus – largely because he stood more properly in the tradition of the previous Jewish scriptures. Akyol puts it that:

> This Way, as James and his fellow believers called it, was opened and defined by Jesus not as a new religion but as an update of Judaism. '[James's] religious beliefs were primarily those of the orthodox Jew of the first century,' an American Christian scholar put it, 'modified little save by the conviction that [Jesus] was the Messiah.' And for both James and his fellow believers at the 'Jerusalem Church,' this Messiah was not God incarnate, but 'the last great Jewish prophet'.[28]

The second important premise in Akyol's argument is that both the Jewish and Gentile communities developed gospels, but that, over time, the Gentile church came to dominate Christianity and shape the formation of the Bible. As a result, the Jewish Christian gospels were either lost or rejected, and today we are left with only remnants of Jewish Christianity in the Bible: most notably the letter of James. According to Akyol, this letter of James remains staunchly anti-Trinitarian – with any hints of worshipping Jesus as divine being later additions.

Third, despite the swift dominance of Gentile Christianity, remnant Jewish Christian communities survived in Judea, and into Arabia. One of these communities was the Ebionites. From early church history we know that the Ebionites represent the sort of 'Jewish Christianity' in mind here: they rejected the teaching of Paul as un-Jewish, denied the divinity of Jesus, and grounded their teaching in the (lost) 'Gospel of the Hebrews'.

Fourth, Akyol sees the parallels between the Jesus of Jewish Christianity and the Muslim Jesus as striking and significant. Indeed, he sees the similarities as so striking as to suggest they are talking about the same person, who follows the same religion. Akyol finds some support for this in scholarship:

27

Robert Eisenman, a prominent biblical scholar, historian, and archeologist, also finds it 'very curious' that 'the key ideology of faith and works together, associated with James in New Testament Scripture, fairly shines through the Koran.' Furthermore, he argues, 'Muslim dietary law is also based on James' directives to overseas communities as delineated in the Book of Acts.'[29]

Fifth, Akyol believes that recognizing Yeshua, the Jewish Christian Jesus, as one and the same as the Islamic Jesus solves many of the Christological conundrums we observed earlier. So, for example, in answer to the question of what theological meaning there is behind the title of Messiah, Islam can simply and happily adopt a fully Jewish Christian Messiah. The Muslim doctrine of Messiah then is

> the very doctrine upheld by Jewish Christians, centuries before Islam. For Jewish Christians, as we saw in the previous chapters, Jesus was the awaited Messiah, but only as the last great Jewish prophet, not as God.[30]

Akyol offers a second example of apparent resolution. So, earlier we found the 'table' miracle problematic due to the Christological claims made in the Eucharist. Akyol suggests that this problem evaporates when we see the Lord's supper through Jewish Christian eyes:

> the unusual Eucharist we see in the Qur'an seems to present Jesus and his disciples in a distinctly Jewish framework. Here we have, one could even say, not a Christian Eucharist but a Jewish-Christian Eucharist… In other words, Ebionites were not celebrating the Eucharist in order to 'eat the body' and 'drink the blood' of the Messiah— an idea totally alien and even repugnant to the Jewish mind. For them, the Last Supper was rather 'a mere remembrance of the table fellowship with Jesus.' It was probably also fashioned on the Jewish Passover, with themes from the Old Testament. So, we can argue that the

ma'ida story in the Qur'an, as a reinterpreted Last Supper, is theologically compatible with the Ebionite version of the Last Supper. It suggests, once again, that Jewish Christianity and Islam are somehow congruous.[31]

The final step in Akyol's argument is to suggest that recognizing Yeshua as the Muslim Messiah removes any (Islamic) theological obstacles to adopting Jesus' ethical teaching for Muslim devotional purposes. He points out that:

> Especially in the Umayyad and early Abbasid era, *Isra'iliyyat* added a lot to Muslim literature and culture, 'flow[ing] into the Muslim lands like a river' as a Turkish scholar poetically notes, 'triggering new crops to grow.'[32]

The *Qisas al-Anbiya* we explored earlier are precisely one type of *Isra'iliyyat*, and so this last step allows us to merge the Jewish Messiah and the Sufi Jesus. Doing so, argues Akyol, provides us with a Muslim Jesus historically and theologically robust enough to serve as a devotionally unifying character between Christians and Muslims.

At face value, this is an appealing argument. If we could properly recognize Yeshua as the true Jesus it does seem to offer intriguing possibilities: for making sense of the emergence of the Muslim Christ; for resolving Christological controversies; and for grounding shared Muslim/Christian devotion. However, before we jump too quickly to adopt this 'unified Muslim Jesus' theory we need to look closely at three important hurdles it must negotiate.

First, we need to make sure we have our history right. Yeshua (or any other Muslim Jesus) is only of use if he really does exist! Even Akyol recognizes that his argument rests on some highly controversial historical scholarship. We need to look more closely at that scholarship to see if his conclusions stand scrutiny. The sorts of questions we will need to ask include: whether Jewish Christianity existed in the form that Akyol suggests; whether Gentile Christianity truly abandoned the historical Jesus; whether the Jewish Christian gospel bore anything more than a hypothetical relation to Islam; and, perhaps most importantly, whether the Bible really was corrupted in the way described.

Second, we need to look closely at whether this Yeshua fares any better than Jesus Son of Mary at negotiating the range of doctrinal controversies that swirl around the Muslim Jesus. This may prove more difficult than Akyol suggests. For a start, the examples he offers as puzzle solutions will need closer examination. More problematically, even if 'Jewish Christianity' existed as described, its Jesus is even more elusive than the Muslim Jesus! As we will see, beyond their denials of Paul and Jesus' divinity, we know virtually nothing about the Ebionites. Their gospels are lost, and we have no evidence whatever that there is any substantial resemblance between their Messiah and any version of the Muslim Jesus. If there is any obvious similarity it is that both these characters are theologically thin. As presented to us in history and the Qur'an, both are elusive figures who take the form of a prophet who preached a simple monotheism. This skeleton is so thin it can – and has - been fleshed out as desired. We have just seen how onto these bare prophetic bones have been happily hung an ascetic, an apologist, a miracle worker, a Jewish prophet and fulfiller of Jewish prophecy, a judgement day executioner, a teacher of ethics, a vicarious sacrifice and a Word and Spirit from God. Perhaps an ordinary prophet can be all these things at once. We will, however, need to be shown just how.

Third, we need to establish – in practical detail – just how any Muslim Jesus might show us the ideal religious way of life. Yeshua's promise in this regard largely stems from his legitimizing the teaching tradition found in the *Qisas al-Anbiya*. While it is true that we find there a rich vein of religious wisdom, we will need to mine that vein carefully to see whether it is rich enough to provide the sort of robust social ethic required to build flourishing communities in today's fraught geo-political climate.

So far, this book has merely introduced us to the Muslim Jesus. Its real work is to explore how this Jesus negotiates these three discussions – and how he does so in comparison to the orthodox Christian Jesus. We begin with the historical.

Part 2

CORRUPTING JESUS?

6

Conspiracy

Everyone loves a good conspiracy theory. As a teenager, one of my favourite books was *The Philadelphia Experiment*. It claimed to be a true expose of a U.S. government coverup of a World War II naval experiment. The story went that Einstein's theories opened the way for the U.S. Navy to develop a device which used magnetism to render the USS *Eldridge* invisible through some sort of teleportation through time and space. The appeal of this theory is obvious! How cool would it be if teleportation was true? Unfortunately, it wasn't.

Sometimes, though, conspiracies are true. In 2006, a US federal court found major tobacco companies guilty of fraud and racketeering. The judges' finding outlined how, over the course of more than 50 years, tobacco companies 'lied, misrepresented, and deceived the American public ... [they] suppressed research, they destroyed documents, they manipulated the use of nicotine so as to increase and perpetuate addiction, they distorted the truth about low-tar and light cigarettes so as to discourage smokers from quitting.'[33] Clearly, when the stakes are high, some people are prepared to go to extraordinary lengths to conspire to shape public narratives away from the truth.

Jesus of Nazareth has attracted more than his fair share of conspiracy theories. Over the years different theorists have claimed that Jesus taught reincarnation but that the church suppressed it, that he married Mary Magadalene who bore him children but that again the church covered it up, and, more recently, that he never existed at all!

At its heart, the Muslim Jesus story involves just such a historical conspiracy. It claims that the mainstream Christian accounts of Jesus' life – the biblical Gospels – were intentionally fabricated. It suggests that somehow, somewhere, someone conspired to corrupt, and cover up, the true story of Jesus. Did this happen?

Before we try to work this out, it is worth pausing for a moment to consider how conspiracy theories operate.

The appeal of conspiracy theories is obvious. There is something exhilarating about the thought we can discover hidden intrigues or sub-plots playing out in our world. It plays into our pride to think that we have exclusive access to privileged knowledge or are clever enough to see through tricks that others are trying to play on us. For cultures like Australia's, it also allows people to justify an anti-authoritarian streak. We like saying things like 'See, I told you those politicians were not trustworthy!'

Accepting these sorts of theories as true, however, carries a few risks. Here are two.

First, conspiracy theories are hard to prove or disprove. Because they hinge upon the idea of a deliberate deception, it means they can cope with being challenged with a lack of evidence. Consider the Philadelphia Experiment. Is there a lack of evidence that this experiment ever took place? That's because it was covered up and the evidence destroyed! Is there contradictory evidence – like the ship not being in the area at the time? That's because the government fabricated records to cover it up! This resilience in the face of missing or contradictory evidence is not a good thing if you are seeking truth.

Second, conspiracy theories are highly vulnerable to confirmation bias. Confirmation bias is when, instead of simply believing things based on where all the evidence naturally points, we go looking for, or only accepting, evidence that supports what we *want* to believe is true. Confirmation bias is a well-recognized phenomenon in all our thinking. So, for example, in one study it was found that 70–80 per cent of drivers believed that they were above average – in the top 50 per cent – behind the wheel. This means around one third of all drivers think they are better than they really are! Conspiracy theories are perfectly set up to affirm our biases. If I desperately want the idea of magnetic teleportation to be real, then I may well cling on to any tiny clues or weak scraps of evidence for the Philadelphia Experiment. If I deeply distrust government authorities, I might enthusiastically jump onto *any* hints I can find that they are deceiving me. A cover-up theory is fertile ground for affirming our treasured biases. This can become truly dangerous ground if the theory – and our belief – is not true.

Now as a religious believer, I am conscious that religious conspiracy theories are at great risk of these sorts of problems. Religious beliefs are usually held very deeply and strongly. They are also beliefs that come with a well-established framework for explaining life, the universe and everything. This framework happily allows us to filter in – or out – any new evidence that comes to hand depending on whether it easily fits our worldview.

Because of this, religious thinkers haven't always had the best track record when it comes to evaluating beliefs held by competing worldviews. Here's one example from a key person in our investigation. Mustafa Akyol first met the Christian Jesus when he was given a New Testament as a gift. Despite various suspicions, he read all the way through to see exactly what it said. Obviously, that's a good move! We *should* carefully examine all the evidence available to us. The problem was that he decided that he would do so using the following method:

> I began underlining the passages of the New Testament that I liked the most with a blue pen while underlining the passages that I found objectionable with a red pen. It soon turned out that I had more blue lines in the gospels, especially in the first three, whereas the epistles of Paul got filled with many red lines. Paul's 'Christology'— a term I would learn later— was just not working for me.[34]

Notice what is happening here. Akyol's initial method was to read the New Testament through an Islamic lens. Anything that fit his Islamic religious worldview was accepted; anything that didn't was rejected. The problem with this approach, of course, is that it doesn't take the New Testament *on its own terms*. It doesn't allow the text to speak for itself, or the reader to have their ideas challenged. Theory-driven approaches to history like this can sometimes deliver interesting findings – Muslims might ask interpretive questions Christians wouldn't dream of – but they need to be a whole lot more sophisticated than 'accepting what I like', and a whole lot more willing to wrestle deeply with those things we find objectionable. In the end, the problem here was that Akyol read the Christian traditions through a religious ideological lens, not a scholarly historical one.

Fortunately, Akyol grew to recognize that his religious framework needs to stand historical scrutiny:

> For Muslims, including myself, this question (of the Gospels) has a metaphysical answer: Islam's origin is divine revelation. The voice that spoke to Muhammad in that cave was really not a demon or a hallucination, but the Angel Gabriel. God had revealed His word to Abraham, Moses, and Jesus before, and He revealed it to Muhammad as well. Thus the parallels between Islam and older monotheisms are easy to explain: they reflect the continuation of the same revealed wisdom that comes from the same God.

> For non-Muslims, however, who would understandably not accept this faith-based answer, the question is how Muhammad accumulated and incorporated the knowledge of older religious traditions into the Qur'an along with his own sayings— which later were collected as the hadiths, making up the secondary textual source of Islam. The question, in other words, is what the 'historical Muhammad' inherited and from whom.[35]

In short, as Akyol delved deeper into his journey to discover the true Jesus he adopted a more sophisticated historical method that allowed his religious convictions about this ancient prophet to be properly questioned.

As we evaluate the Muslim Jesus conspiracy we will need to do the same. Perhaps the conspiracy is real, and the traditional

Christian Jesus is a fabrication. To buy in, though, we will need to make sure the evidence points obviously to conspiracy. Allegations, hints, possibilities, unexplained mysteries, historical gaps, and mere speculations will not be enough. We will need concrete evidence. Indeed, we will need concrete evidence for the *cover-up itself*. Preferably, we will need trustworthy accounts of the actual collusions to conspire – including the names of conspirators – as well as concrete evidence of manuscript destruction/manipulation.

This will take a little work because, while virtually all Muslims agree that there is a conspiracy, what they haven't agreed upon is just who it was perpetrated the crime. Let's start with what the Qur'an has to say about the matter.

7

The Christians

Over the years, virtually all my Muslim friends have confidently assured me that the Bible has been deliberately corrupted. Heck, virtually every Muslim taxi driver I have met has confidently assured me the Bible has been deliberately corrupted! The interesting thing about this is that none of my friends (or drivers) has been able to tell me the story of exactly how it was changed, or who was responsible. For most Muslims, the idea is simply an Islamic truism. It is an article of faith, or a doctrine, that has been passed on by their religious authorities. But, if the Christian tradition concerning Jesus was changed, who were the culprits? The first clues Islam provides as to who twisted the accounts of Jesus come directly out of the Qur'an. There we are told that Christians have a track-record of corrupting God's words.

The Qur'anic claim

The Islamic scriptures make the weighty claim that the Jews and Christians had a history of *distorting* God's words. So, in Surah al-Baqara we find:

> a party of them used to hear the words of Allah and then distort it after they had understood it while they were knowing. (Q2.75)

Similarly, in Surah al-Nisa we read:

> Among the Jews are those who distort words from their places … (Q4.46)

To be sure, in these verses at least, the Qur'an is not outlining a conspiracy theory per se; it is more like a conspiracy allegation. Here, no story is told, no manuscripts are referred to, no distortions are outlined, no culprits are named, and no dates are given. Indeed, even the type of distortion described by the Qur'an is unclear. This question has been debated fiercely by scholars throughout history. Some have thought it is corrupt interpretation or teaching on view here (*tahrīf al-maʿnā*), others have argued instead for corruption of the text (*tahrīf al-nass*)? It is probably fair to say that most scholars throughout history have taken it that the verses refer to distorted *teaching*, rather than distorted *texts*. In any case, one thing *is* clear: when it came to deliberately distorting God's message, Christians had form. So, the first building block of the theory is that Christians could not be trusted with the story of Jesus.

Islamic logic

Wherever scholarship landed on these verses, it is undeniable that over time most Muslim thinkers have indeed come to believe that the Christian Gospel texts themselves *were* corrupted. That is, whether the Qur'an mentioned it or not, some sort of *tahrif al-nass* took place. They do so primarily based on Islamic logic.

Here's what I mean by Islamic logic. Most Muslims should have no problem agreeing with the following five claims:

- The Qur'an denies Jesus' death on the cross and his divinity.
- The Qur'an affirms the 'gospel' (*injeel*) to be scripture.
- The Qur'an affirms that some Christians distorted the teaching about Jesus.
- The Qur'an affirms that some Christians believe untrue things about Jesus.
- The biblical Gospels affirm Jesus' death on a cross, and (arguably) affirm Jesus' divinity.

The most obvious way for all these claims to fit together – that is, to all be true – is for the gospel of the Qur'an to be different from the biblical Gospels, due to Christian distortion. That's just simple Islamic reasoning.

One really interesting quirk of history is that it took the early Muslims a long time to outline this logical argument. Why? Because it seems they had little idea that the Christian Gospel texts contradicted the Qur'an about Jesus. How could this be? Earlier we saw that pre-Islamic Arabs were familiar with stories of the Christian Jesus. That doesn't mean, however, that they were familiar with the Christian Gospel *texts*. Every indication is that they had very little access to the Gospels themselves. This makes sense. Most Arabs were illiterate, almost none would have owned a Bible, and, unless you were a Christian, you were unlikely to have spent much time hearing one systematically read out loud. Also, at that time there were no Arabic translations of the Bible (as far as we know). Any text would have been in Greek or Hebrew or Syriac. With this understandable ignorance of the Christian Gospels, any early Muslim could happily go on believing that the Christian gospel affirmed Islam, and that the Qur'an was rebuking Christian teachers, not its Scriptures.

Once Islam had properly conquered the Middle East, all that changed. The Muslim empire drew Christian communities under its wings and over time Muslims and Christians started to work together, study together, teach at universities together and publicly debate religion together. It was only then that Muslims started to read the actual texts of the Christian Gospels in detail. It was only then they realized these Gospels contradicted Islamic teaching about Jesus. So, it was only then they began to use Islamic reasoning to argue that the Christian Gospels *must* have been changed.

For many Muslims, this Islamic logic is all that we need to know the truth about Jesus. If the Qur'an is the Word of God, then the only possible solution to the puzzle is that the biblical Gospels were corrupted. It does not matter which Christians perpetrated the corruption, nor how, when or where the corruption took place. All we need to know for the purposes of faith is that they *were* corrupted, and that Christians had a dodgy track record when it comes to deliberate distortion. Even without naming the individual culprits, it's an open-and-shut case.

Except it's only an open-and-shut *religious* case. It only works if you accept the Islamic logic that frames the case. Christians are highly unlikely to accept this logic – and historians certainly won't. To convince them, the Muslim Jesus conspiracy will need to make an *historical* case for corruption. It is not enough to simply cast doubt on Christian trustworthiness: we will need to find evidence of corrupted manuscripts. Ideally, we should find a culprit, or culprits, with this textual 'blood' on their hands. Unsurprisingly, over the years many Christians pointed this out, and so, obligingly, Muslim thinkers went about developing the theory in more historical detail.

8
The Apostles

In a culture too often being fed the simplistic nonsense that religion has always been a fundamental cause of world conflict, it might come as a surprise to know that throughout history Christians and Muslims engaged in healthy, substantial, and rigorous scholarly debate. Unquestionably that was regularly the case under the Muslim empires of the Middle Ages. Once Muslim scholars got their hands on the Christian Gospels they scoured them to see how they exhibited the sort of corruption described by Islamic logic. Soon they found some prime suspects among the Christians: Jesus' apostles themselves.

Ibn Hazm's theory

In the Middle Ages, various Muslim apologists began to try to describe how the Jesus conspiracy had played out. Influential among these early theorists was the Spanish Muslim polymath, Ibn Hazm. He attempted to rigorously investigate both the *content* of the Christian Gospels as well as their process of *transmission* through history. His conclusion was that the Jesus story was corrupted because his apostles were 'accursed liars'.

When Ibn Hazm examined the Christian scriptures one thing immediately jumped out at him: The Gospels present as works of history. He identified the authors of these histories as the first evangelists – by which he meant Matthew, Mark, Luke, and John – and recognized that each of their accounts combined their own individual eye-witness experience of Jesus with accepted oral traditions circulating about Jesus at the time. Regarding these histories of Jesus, Ibn Hazm made three claims. Two concern the contents of the texts, one concerns the handling of the texts themselves.

First, he observed what he saw to be numerous historical contradictions between the different accounts of Jesus' life. These include things like, for example, how the calling of the apostles to follow Jesus reads differently in each of the Gospels. This led him straightforwardly to the conclusion that, for every contradiction, at least one of the Gospels is not true.

Ibn Hazm's second claim flowed directly from the first: if the Gospels contradict each other, then someone is deliberately not telling the truth. Indeed, his claim is much stronger than that. He believed that since the Gospels were riddled with contradictions the only sensible conclusion is that they were authored by accursed liars.

Intriguingly, he made a third claim to do with the reliability of the manuscripts themselves. He argued that, since Christians suffered heavy persecution for the first three hundred years of Christianity, they would have found it difficult to safeguard their sacred texts.

What can we say of this theory?

Clearly, Ibn Hazm is correct in recognizing the Gospels as human works of history. Whichever way Christians see God as being involved in their production, Ibn Hazm affirms the traditional Christian idea that the four biblical Gospels were intentionally written down as records of the apostles' eye-witness experience of Jesus.

Regarding contradictions, I want to say this: Christians and Muslims have been flinging accusations of contradictions at each other's scriptures from time immemorial. In my view, this time-honoured tradition nearly always suffers from serious problems. Far too often it reads the texts superficially and simplistically. It is usually deeply skeptical and ungenerous. It often goes looking for contradictions, and not harmony. It rarely acknowledges the full range of possible explanations. It mostly avoids taking seriously how adherents of that scripture have read the text or made sense of apparent tensions. It really does seem patronizing to suggest to either Christians or Muslims that they would happily accept scriptures filled with obvious contradictions, and bare-faced lies.

Having said that, I suggest that none of the supposed contradictions mentioned by Ibn Hazm are devastating for the historical reliability of the Gospels. All have been recognized by Christians from day one, and all have sensible explanations. Indeed, professional historians regard the different takes on Jesus' life from the four Gospels not as evidence of error, but instead as evidence of historicity! To show this requires a whole book of its own. Because of this, I'll simply refer interested readers to read *Is the New Testament History*, by Dr Paul Barnett, and move on.[36]

One really interesting thing about Ibn Hazm is that he was among the first Muslims to try to describe the process by which the first Christians preserved their Gospels. It is indeed true that they were persecuted heavily by the Roman Empire. What isn't true is that this persecution meant they couldn't look after their Scriptures.

To see why I say this, it's time to tell the story of how the church came to have four Gospels. What I'll outline is the traditional story. It is the story accepted by mainstream historical scholars. It is a story best told, in many people's opinion, by Dr Martin Hengel in his brilliant book *The Four Gospels and the One Gospel of the Lord Jesus Christ*. The story, in a nutshell, and in my words, goes as follows.

The four Gospels

When I lived in Egypt, I visited the Coptic cathedral in Alexandria. Wandering around I came upon a plaque that listed all the Archbishops who had led that community of believers down through the years. To my astonishment, the list went way back in time. In fact, it went all the way back to the beginnings of Christianity: the first name on the list was the evangelist Mark. According to the traditions Mark was one of Jesus' disciples, who became the apostle Peter's travelling companion, scribe, and translator. Mark travelled to Egypt preaching the gospel, established a church there, and remained as the leader of this fledgling community. Sometime during his ministry, Mark's own eye-witness testimony to the events around Jesus' life, as well as his record of Peter's apostolic preaching, was committed to writing. This document is what we now call the Gospel of Mark. Perhaps – like in the case of the Qur'an and the companions of Muhammad – this shift from oral to written testimony was due to Mark's advancing age and the risk of losing the authoritative witness. In any case, centred around Mark's teaching, Alexandria soon became a burgeoning hub of Christian teaching and scholarship.

Just like this, the story of how Christianity ended up with four Gospels is a story that follows the *journeys* of the apostles, the *communities* they established and the *libraries* that developed as these communities collected as much of the apostolic testimony they could.

The central characters, of course, are Jesus' apostles. The term apostle literally means 'sent one', and the story goes that after his resurrection Jesus commissioned his twelve disciples to take his message to the 'ends of the earth' (Acts 1.8). Now not any old disciple could be an apostle. To qualify you needed to be both an eye-witness of Jesus' life, as well as personally commissioned by him to do the job. In short, in the time before there were any written gospels, the 'apostles' were those entrusted with the authoritative, oral, eye-witness accounts of Jesus.

After their commissioning, and over time, the apostles, with their scribes, travelled out across the ancient world spreading this word. As in Alexandria, wherever they went churches were established, and over time the apostles became the leaders of these communities. In broad brush-strokes, the tradition records that Matthew and James led and testified in Judea and Syria, Paul (and his scribe Luke) led and testified in Asia and Rome, Peter and his scribe Mark led and testified in Asia and Africa, and John led and testified in Asia.

Perhaps this rings a bell for readers regarding something interesting we saw earlier. The Muslim historian al-Tabari described the spread of the gospel like this:

> Those whom Jesus Son of Mary sent, both disciples and those who came after them, in the land were: Peter the disciple and Paul with him, (Paul belonged to the followers and was not a disciple) to Rome; Andrew and Matthew to the land of the cannibals; Thomas to the land of Babel which is the land of the East; Philip to Carthage which is Africa; John to Ephesus the city of the young men of the cave; James to Jerusalem which is Aelia the city of the sanctuary; Bartholomew to Arabia which is the land of the Hijaz; Simon to the land of the Berbers; Judah who was not one of the disciples was put in the place of Judas.

This is, in virtually every respect, an identical account to the traditional Christian one. Where ever al-Tabari derived his account from, he clearly had no problem endorsing both the events and the people involved. It is worth wondering: if the apostles were such obvious liars, wouldn't al-Tabari have mentioned it? Either way, back to our story ...

Over time, four of these apostolic centres committed the authoritative oral testimony to writing. These texts are what we now call the four Gospels: Matthew, John, Mark (with the authority of Peter), and Luke (with the authority of Paul). Of course, this process was not simultaneous or independent. The communities were not isolated, and the apostles travelled widely between them. The apostles had a shared experience and testimony, and scholarship has long recognized that Mark's Gospel (containing the testimony of Peter) was written first, and that Matthew and Luke relied on it as a source for their own Gospels. The Gospels were written in various places, and for different audiences: Mark (as we've seen) was written in Egypt, Matthew in Judea, Luke in Italy, and John in Asia. This is part of the reason they tell the story of Jesus' life in diverse ways and with different emphases.

Once these Gospels had been produced in their different communities, something very significant happened: the communities started sharing their Gospels with each other. Copies were made and sent around the different churches around the Mediterranean world – to both the major centres and smaller churches.

Something else important happened too. The apostles didn't just write Gospels – they wrote letters as well. Again, these letters were written all around the Mediterranean. In fact – and this will be very important later – the letters we have in the New Testament originated from the *same four apostolic communities as the Gospels*. So, we have letters from Paul (linked to Luke), James (linked to Matthew), John and Peter. Again, the communities that received these letters made copies and shared them around.

So, by the end of the first century CE the situation was that Christian communities all around the ancient world were developing their own libraries containing Gospels and letters from the apostles. Not every library would have had every text. Some of the big communities, like in Alexandria and Rome, were in a place to collect them all. Over time, the Roman collection would come to be regarded as the most comprehensive and authoritative. And it was that collection that formed what we call the New Testament. Despite Rome taking the lead – and despite later conspiracy theories! – there wasn't much controversy over just which Gospels and letters were considered apostolic. History records that the churches were extraordinarily conservative in deciding what to accept as carrying eye-witness authority. There was, for the most part, deep consensus: the collection in Rome didn't differ from the collection in Alexandria or the collection in Constantinople. The story of the Christian Gospels, then, is a story of four communities, in four very different parts of the world, sharing their apostolic testimonies among themselves – and a vast number of smaller communities.

There is lots more to say about this of course. Most obviously, the story will need to include details of how other gospels like the 'Gospel to the Hebrews' fit in. We'll come to that soon.

For now, let's get back to Ibn Hazm's conspiracy theory. Recall that his claim was that persecution meant that Christians couldn't look after the Gospel texts. Certainly, it is true that persecution of Christians happened across the Roman empire. However, history records this persecution as sporadic. There is no record of the simultaneous, systematic attack on every church in every place in the empire. Indeed, the sheer size, complexity, and careful nature of the global network of church libraries meant it would have been virtually impossible to systematically or deliberately destroy or corrupt all the texts. On top of that, outside of allegations like Ibn Hazm's we have no record either of the church struggling to maintain their libraries, or of the Roman Empire conspiring to destroy them.

The apostles might still be suspects, but the case for them being 'accursed liars' or on the run from persecution falls short. It simply doesn't line up with the evidence.

9

The Council of Nicea

One of the hallmarks of many conspiracy theories is that they describe society's formal powers and authorities as those orchestrating the cover-up. Over time, the Muslim Jesus conspiracy theory identified just such an institutional culprit conspiring to adjust the Gospels to their own ends: The Council of Nicaea.

Unlike the situation with Islam, it took a very long time for the Christian church to be in the situation where it had strong centralized authorities with the sort of political clout to pull off a religious plot. However, by the early fourth century two things had happened. The first was that the Christian church had become the religious institution at the centre of two great empires: the Roman and the Byzantine. What we now call the Roman Catholic (or Western) church was centred in Rome; what we now call the Orthodox (or Eastern) church was centred in Constantinople (now called Istanbul).

The second was that Jesus had become a controversial figure. Nearly every Christian church was teaching that he was divine – the problem was there was great disagreement about just how that worked. Debates about the person of Jesus raged: the so-called Christological controversies. These debates led to the church calling together various councils to make authoritative declarations about church doctrine. One such council took place in Nicaea, in 325 CE. One of the things affirmed at this council was the legitimacy of the four traditional Gospels. Both the council discussion, and the climate of controversy seem pregnant with conspiratorial possibilities. In line with this a new theory came to capture the Muslim imagination: at Nicaea the truth about Jesus was covered up. This claim is at least as old as Abd al-Jabbar in the tenth century CE. One of the writers to popularize this theory recently was Pakistani apologist Muhammad 'Ata Ur-Rahim.

Ur-Rahim's theory

Ur-Rahim has outlined his theory of how the Council of Nicaea distorted the Gospels in his popular book, *Jesus, A Prophet of Islam*. Here is his description of how things played out:

> The Gospel of Barnabas is the only known Gospel written by a disciple of Jesus, that is, by a man who spent most of his actual time in the company of Jesus during the three years in which he was delivering his message. He therefore had direct experience and knowledge of Jesus' teaching, unlike all the authors of the four accepted Gospels. ... The Gospel of Barnabas was accepted as a Canonical Gospel in the churches of Alexandria up until 325 A.D. ... In 325 A.D., the famous Council of Nicaea was held. The Doctrine of the Trinity was declared to be the official doctrine of the Pauline Church, and one of the consequences of this decision was that out of the three hundred or so Gospels extant at that time, four were chosen as the official Gospels of the Church. The remaining Gospels, including the Gospel of Barnabas, were ordered to be destroyed completely. It was also decided that all Gospels written in Hebrew should be destroyed. An edict was issued stating that anyone found in possession of an unauthorized Gospel was to be put to death. ... Pope Damascus (304–384 A.D.) who became Pope in 366 A.D., is recorded as having issued a decree that the Gospel of Barnabas should not be read...[37]

Three core claims can be distilled from this:

1. There were originally very many legitimate gospels, including the Gospel of Barnabas.
2. To affirm Jesus' divinity, the Council of Nicaea adopted Matthew, Mark, Luke, and John alone as legitimate Gospels.
3. The Council ordered all other gospels destroyed or repudiated.

It is a mystery to me just how this theory managed to gain any traction at all! That's because all its core claims are patently false. Even without looking at the proceedings of the council it is nonsense to suggest it played a role in shaping the Bible. The key evidence for this is that half the church wasn't even at the council! It was only a council of the Eastern Church. Aside from a few observers, the Western church wasn't even represented. This means the council was not in the position to decide anything about the shape of the Bible even if it wanted to! Not only that, the Gospels in the Bible remained unchanged from before and after the council, and in both Eastern and Western churches.

In any case, the proceedings of the council are available, and they are embarrassing reading for any supporters of this theory. They make very clear that the Gospel of Barnabas was never mentioned, let alone banned, at the Council of Nicaea. Indeed, it wasn't mentioned by Pope Damascus, or by anyone else for that matter. That's because until the fifteenth century CE there is no record of there being a Gospel of Barnabas at all.

The Gospel of Barnabas

Despite its claims to legitimacy having gained traction in the popular Muslim imagination, I do not propose to waste many words on discussing the Gospel of Barnabas. This is because, put simply, it is almost certainly a fake. Don't take my word for it though. Listen to Akyol:

> ...the Gospel of Barnabas ... is considered by most scholars as a pseudepigraphal work, indeed a pious forgery, apparently written in the fifteenth century by some unknown Muslim author to help support the Qur'anic view of Jesus.[38]

This means that the Nicaea conspiracy – ur-Rahim's version at least – bears no historical scrutiny at all. The Gospel of Barnabas is almost certainly a fraud masquerading as an original.

I am genuinely astonished at the charges laid upon the Council of Nicaea by Muslim apologists. All the evidence points to the case being thrown out of court and so, sensibly, many Muslims have done just that. Doing so, however, has left Muslim conspiracy theorists with seemingly only one remaining conspiratorial suspect: the apostle Paul.

10

Paul

Paul of Tarsus has long been viewed by Muslims as a key conspirator in the plot to corrupt the true story of Jesus. The very early Muslim historian, Sayf ibn Umar al-Tamimi, for one, held him to be responsible for propagating the teaching that God made Himself manifest in Jesus.[39]

If the four Gospels we have *are* inauthentic then Paul appears an ideal suspect for substituting them for the originals. His letters are generally regarded as the earliest writings in the New Testament – they are almost certainly earlier than the Gospels. Perhaps it is possible that his teaching gained enough popularity to influence the early church's selection of the Gospels about Jesus. This is precisely what Akyol is arguing. His case against Paul rests on these three allegations:

1. Paul wasn't a proper apostle because he was not an eye-witness of Jesus' life.
2. Paul wasn't properly aligned with the Jerusalem church.
3. Paul preached a different message from the Jerusalem church.

Let's consider each claim in turn. First, notice something about where Akyol is turning to for evidence of his claims: the New Testament. Akyol's description of Paul's experiences of Jesus is sourced solely from the New Testament texts; his assessment that Paul was some sort of rogue apostle is similarly derived exclusively from the Bible; as is his determination that Paul's message was different from the Jerusalem church. The reason for this is straightforward: the New Testament is the *only* primary historical source we have for knowing what went on at the time.

There's literally *nowhere else* that Akyol can find evidence for his theory.

This leaves Akyol's case with a glaring problem: his corruption theory doesn't trust the Christian Bible to be a reliable witness. In short, he is assuming the truth of the New Testament to argue for the corruption of the New Testament! The only way I can see around this problem is for Akyol to accept the truth of *some* parts of the New Testament – those telling the story of Paul – to argue for the corruption of *other* parts – those telling the story of Jesus. Akyol doesn't justify his grounds for choosing just which parts are reliable, and I can't see a sensible way to do so. However, for sake of argument, let's run with it and see whether the biblical account of Paul and the early church really tells the story of an unqualified, rebellious, conspirator.

An eye-witness?

Regarding Paul's apostolic credentials Akyol says this:

> ...there is something mind-boggling about this most influential apostle of Jesus: he had never seen Jesus with his own eyes or heard him speak with his own ears. He was not a member of the Twelve who followed Jesus throughout his ministry. He was not even a member of the 'Jerusalem Church' that was led by James and others who knew Jesus in person.[40]

> ...Paul believed that he did not need such a natural acquaintance with Jesus at all. He rather had a supernatural acquaintance, which was far superior. 'I want you to know, brothers and sisters, that the gospel I preached is not of human origin,' hence he wrote in his Epistle to the Galatians. 'I did not receive it from any man, nor was I taught it; rather, I received it by revelation from Jesus Christ.'[41]

Now Akyol is correct, of course, that Paul is unique as an apostle. No, he wasn't one of the 'twelve'. No, he wasn't an eye-witness to

Jesus earthly ministry. And no, he hadn't been there when Jesus was crucified. It is true, too, that the first, formative encounter Paul had with Jesus was a supernatural one: he received a spiritual vision of the resurrected Jesus. All that is correct.

I don't see, though, why this should be a problem for a Muslim. Surely any Muslim can accept a supernatural vision as evidence of divine calling. Isn't the very nature of divine revelation that it is supernatural? Isn't all prophecy supernatural? Tellingly, too, isn't this exactly what they claim happened with Muhammad? Isn't the Qur'an supposed to be the product of supernatural experiences? If Akyol wants to rule out Paul as a legitimate vehicle of divine revelation, simply by virtue of the nature of his experience, then that places Muhammad on very shaky ground too.

No. For any theist, the type of revelation Paul received is irrelevant to his apostolic claim. All that matters is that Paul's experience was real, and truly involved Jesus commissioning him. If this was the case – and Akyol never suggests it wasn't – then who are we to suggest Paul's apostolic role was not legitimate?

A rogue apostle?

The next claim to consider is that Paul was disconnected from the original, faithful Jerusalem church. Akyol describes it like this:

Paul developed his own theology independently of the 'Jerusalem Church' led by James. After his miraculous conversion on the way to Damascus, he spent three years in 'Arabia,' an imprecise location which probably corresponds to modern-day Jordan. Here, his Christian faith began to be formed – all by himself, for he had decided 'not to consult any human being.' Only after that did Paul visit Jerusalem for two weeks, there to meet only Peter and, much more briefly, James.[42]

Again, Akyol makes some accurate observations about Paul's early life of faith. Sure, Paul wasn't converted into the Jerusalem church, it was indeed three years before he met the apostle Peter, and sure, Paul didn't immediately consult the Jerusalem apostles before accepting his commissioning from Jesus. All this is a fair reading of Paul's personal testimony in his letter to the Galatians. The problem is it is not the whole story. We know so much more of Paul's life that calls into question any notion that he was an independent operator. There are extra – and relevant – details we can glean from Paul's story in the book of Acts.

So, immediately after his conversion, Paul was met by a Christian called Ananias. This man, too, had received a vision of Jesus telling him that Paul was a genuine believer – indeed an 'instrument' in Jesus' hands to take the gospel to the world. It was Ananias who introduced Paul to the (already established) Damascene church, which welcomed him into their community. Later, though, Paul did travel to meet the apostles in the Jerusalem church. Initially, they were reluctant to meet him due to his past life as a persecutor of Christians. However, once again, Paul was introduced, and commended personally to the apostles, by a senior member of the Jerusalem church called Barnabas. The book of Acts makes it clear that the Jerusalem church accepted Paul as legitimate – so legitimate in fact that he spent his time 'coming and going with them in Jerusalem speaking boldly in the name of the Lord' (Acts 9.28).

Later, as Akyol recognizes, Paul embarked on three long missionary journeys. All these journeys were commissioned, endorsed, supported, and celebrated by the Judean church. If Paul had been, or over time had become, a theological rebel then why were the apostles happy to send him out as a missionary not once, not twice, but three times?

Another nail in the coffin of any idea that Paul was rogue is found in another, entirely independent piece of evidence: one of the apostle Peter's personal letters. In his second letter he wrote:

> ...just as our beloved brother Paul also wrote to you according to the wisdom given him, as he does in all his letters when he speaks in them of these matters. There are some things in them that are hard to understand, which the ignorant and unstable

twist to their own destruction, as they do the other Scriptures. (2 Peter 3.15–16)

This short passage shows that the apostle Peter – arguably the greatest of the apostles – regarded Paul not simply as a genuine, orthodox Christian, but as God's legitimate mouthpiece for penning Scripture.

There's yet another interesting clue that Paul was in lockstep with the Jerusalem church. In one of Paul's letter (I Corinthians) he outlines his gospel message about Jesus like this:

Now I would remind you, brothers, of the gospel I preached to you, which you received, in which you stand, and by which you are being saved, if you hold fast to the word I preached to you – unless you believed in vain. For I delivered to you as of first importance what I also received: that Christ died for our sins in accordance with the Scriptures, that he was buried, that he was raised on the third day in accordance with the Scriptures, and that he appeared to Cephas, then to the twelve. Then he appeared to more than five hundred brothers at one time, most of whom are still alive, though some have fallen asleep. Then he appeared to James, then to all the apostles. Last of all, as to one untimely born, he appeared also to me. (1 Cor 15.1–8)

Here Paul is appealing to James, and five hundred members of the Jerusalem church, as witness that he is preaching the correct message about Jesus. He deliberately mentions that most of them are still alive. Why? To make the point that if any of his readers doubt the accuracy of his teaching about the events of Jesus' life and death and resurrection they can go to Jerusalem and ask the eye-witnesses – including James! Why would he do this if there had been a split between the Jewish and Gentile churches? Why would he appeal to James if James disapproved of his portrayal of Jesus? Surely, he wouldn't.

When all this evidence is laid on the table we can see that Paul's private, supernatural conversion and commissioning was fully embraced by James and the Judean church – of which Paul became an active member and teacher. This does not read like the story of a rebel.

A corrupter?

There is one part of Paul's story, though, where he does get a little feisty and combative with the Jerusalem church. The Book of Acts records a dispute arising over whether (or not) Gentiles were supposed to keep the same religious law that the Jews were given in the Old Testament. This dispute was real, and so pastorally tricky that a substantial part of the New Testament is devoted to it.

Akyol identifies this debate accurately, but goes on to suggest that there is more going on than meets the eye:

> From the Acts and other books of the New Testament, this whole tension between Paul and the 'Judaizers' first seems to be only about the application of Mosaic Law. But there might well be another major issue: theology, including Christology, or the views about the nature and meaning of Christ.[43]

So, despite the presenting problem being the place of law in the Christian life, Akyol feels that there is an underlying disagreement to do with the person of Jesus. In support of this he argues that:

> The reason why Paul needed to justify himself so insistently… was probably because his 'gospel' was in some conflict with the one upheld by the original Jesus movement in Jerusalem. (p.42)

Let's get this straight. Contrary to the plain reading of the text, Akyol takes it that the New Testament *probably* or *might well* be pointing to Paul preaching a different message – a different Jesus. Okay. The first question to ask is this: If this is only a possibility, then just how likely or probable does he think this is? To my mind, extremely unlikely. Some further questions will reveal why.

So, if Paul taught a conflicting message, then why do we have no record of the twelve apostles challenging *anything* Paul said about Jesus the person, or his encounter with Him? Or, if Paul preached a different message then why does the Gospel that is historically connected to Paul – Luke's Gospel – bear deep similarity to the Gospel of Mark (connected to Peter) and, more importantly, the Gospel of Matthew (connected to the Jerusalem church)? And again, if Paul believed in a different Jesus to the Jerusalem, then why did they keep sending him out as a missionary?

Akyol's argument, then, is weak, and unsurprisingly it is not popular in historical scholarship. The one Christian scholar he invites to the witness stand is liberal Protestant theologian Ferdinand Christian Baur. Akyol summarizes that:

> Once the subjective narrative of the Acts— and the traditional Christian imagination that was built upon it— was left aside, and Paul's own letters were read carefully, Baur argued, the real tension showed up— an argument that, to date, has been admittedly controversial.[44]

Akyol's final concession is telling. Baur's argument, like Akyol's is admittedly controversial because it is pure speculation. All the biblical evidence (that is, all the evidence we have!) is pointing in another direction.

In the end, Akyol's case against Paul suffers a fatal flaw. Put simply, it relies on a hostile witness. Akyol tries to twist the words of the New Testament to portray Paul as a conspirator, but in the end his argument is too selective and too speculative to be persuasive. Instead, the plain reading of the biblical story of Paul presents us with a man remarkably like Muhammad in many ways: a man claiming to be a divinely appointed messenger who was accepted as such by his religious community. To claim otherwise is to violate the text.

Perhaps Paul did preach a different Jesus, but there is no evidence for that in the Bible. To establish it happened we will need to find some more witnesses – from outside the New Testament: more witnesses to what Paul did or didn't say, and more witnesses to describe just how he managed to persuade the original Jerusalem (and Judean) churches to radically corrupt their gospel. Unless these external witnesses are found, the conspiracy seems to me to be extremely improbable.

Funnily enough, this leaves me agreeing with Akyol about Paul in one important respect. He says that:

> At the end of the day, it seems astonishing how the vision of Paul, a man who had never seen or heard Jesus with his earthly eyes and ears, defined the Christ to the world and built the foundation of the greatest religion that has ever existed.[45]

Yes! It would have been incredibly astonishing for Paul, alone, to have defined Jesus to the world. The reason the religion of Christianity grew so great, of course, is that he didn't. He was simply one eye-witness among many.

11

The Ebionites

There is another important group of people involved in the Muslim conspiracy theory: the witnesses whose testimony was supposedly covered up. According to Akyol, the original, true Christians were: centred in Jerusalem; followed James, the brother of Jesus, as their leader; denied Jesus' divinity; and, held possession of an uncorrupted gospel. As this story goes, Paul led an aberrant 'Gentile' Christianity into ascendancy in such a way that, over time, these first Jewish Christians were marginalized, silenced and effectively written out of history – their gospel texts with them. Despite this, a few remnant communities, and texts, survived for enough centuries to leave us with just enough clues for us to establish the existence of the plot.

Now, it does appear possible that very early on there might have been a substantial split between Jewish and Gentile Christians in Jerusalem. The relationship between Jewish and Gentile Christians is one of the central themes of the New Testament and we know for certain there were religious disputes over just what role, if any, the Jewish law had to play in Christian faith. It is unquestionable, too, that early Christianity was diverse. There were many sects, and some were distinctly Jewish in their adherence to the traditional Law. It is also the case that these different groups often had diverse understandings of how to make the most sense of the person of Jesus. None of this is controversial. Christians have known these things from the beginning – and have not sought to cover them up.

The crucial question, then, is this: did James really lead an original Jewish Christianity that was crushed almost out of existence? And did the Gentile church orchestrate a massive cover-up of this event?

The evidence that Akyol musters for this conspiracy centres on a Jewish Christian group called the Ebionites. In his telling, the Ebionites were a remnant of true Jewish Christianity who faithfully clung on to the teaching of James through preserving an uncorrupted gospel – the Gospel of the Hebrews. Indeed, his claim is that these steadfast few preserved not simply the testimony of the true Jesus, but the thread of proper historical mono-theism that traced all the way from Abraham to Muhammad:

> …Islam does not simply begin with the Prophet Muhammad in seventh-century Arabia but is rather rooted in former manifestations of the Abrahamic archetype, from Abraham to Moses, from James the Just to the Ebionites… [appreciating this] would help build, at the very least, a deeper, wider, and wiser Muslim historical imagination.[46]

Akyol suggests that his telling of history is deeper, wider and wiser than that of the traditional Christian story. I want to suggest, instead, that it is merely more imaginative.

The key problem for Akyol's case is that we know so little of the Ebionites. Nearly everything history tells us about them is found in two, short, ancient reports. These texts are so short, in fact, that we can easily find space here to include them in full.

The first, very brief, reference comes from the works of Irenaeus. This early priest (he was taught by the apostle John's disciple, Polycarp) mentioned in passing that:

> Those who are called Ebionites accept that God made the world. However, their opinions with respect to the Lord are quite similar to those of Cerinthus and Carpocrates. They use Matthew's gospel only, and repudiate the Apostle Paul, maintaining that he was an apostate from the Law.[47]

The second, slightly more detailed description is found in the later history of Eusebius. He finds them worthy of the following report:

Chapter XXVII *The Heresy of the Ebionites.*
1. The evil demon, however, being unable to tear certain others

from their allegiance to the Christ of God, yet found them susceptible in a different direction, and so brought them over to his own purposes. The ancients quite properly called these men Ebionites, because they held poor and mean opinions concerning Christ.

2. For they considered him a plain and common man, who was justified only because of his superior virtue, and who was the fruit of the intercourse of a man with Mary. In their opinion the observance of the ceremonial law was altogether necessary, on the ground that they could not be saved by faith in Christ alone and by a corresponding life.

3. There were others, however, besides them, that were of the same name, but avoided the strange and absurd beliefs of the former and did not deny that the Lord was born of a virgin and of the Holy Spirit. But nevertheless, inasmuch as they also refused to acknowledge that he pre-existed, being God, Word, and Wisdom, they turned aside into the impiety of the former, especially when they, like them, endeavored to observe strictly the bodily worship of the law.

4. These men, moreover, thought that it was necessary to reject all the epistles of the apostle, whom they called an apostate from the law; and they used only the so-called Gospel according to the Hebrews and made small account of the rest.

5. The Sabbath and the rest of the discipline of the Jews they observed just like them, but at the same time, like us, they celebrated the Lord's days as a memorial of the resurrection of the Saviour.

6. Wherefore, in consequence of such a course they received the name of Ebionites, which signified the poverty of their understanding. For this is the name by which a poor man is called among the Hebrews.[48]

Some things in these two reports line up nicely with the Muslim Jesus conspiracy: the Ebionites were Jewish followers of Jesus who clearly denied his divinity and prioritized obedience to Jewish law.

They also seem to reject the teaching of Paul but accept the teaching of the Gospel of Matthew/the Hebrews.

Some important things, however, are missing. Significantly, there is no mention of James and no sense of any formal link to the Jerusalem church. Indeed, there is nothing here that places the Ebionites within the early church at all. These precious few details outline nothing of who they were, where were they from, or who their leaders were, or what connection, if any, they had with the Jerusalem church? We are told nothing of how significant they were, and nothing of whether, or not, they were marginalized, oppressed or silenced – apart from them being regarded as religiously impoverished. In short, we have no sense of their *story*.

For Akyol's conspiracy theory to be sustained we need to be able to say for certain that the Ebionites were properly an apostolic community – indeed an original and true apostolic community – and that this was covered up. Nothing in these tiny glimpses into their history shows this to be the case. Except, perhaps, one: their adherence to the Gospel of the Hebrews. If this gospel can be shown to be true, original, and apostolic, then the Ebionites might just be the remnant of true Christianity. It is upon this one remaining thread that the Muslim Jesus conspiracy hangs.

12
The Gospel of the Hebrews

There is one key piece of the Muslim Jesus conspiracy that is unquestionably true: there were indeed 'Jewish Christian' gospels floating around the ancient world that didn't make it into the Bible we have today. The conspiracy argues the church presented us with the wrong Jesus by deliberately selecting four *inauthentic* biographies of his life, instead of the accurate accounts recorded in the Jewish Christian gospels. Is this what really happened?

To answer to that question, we will need to look closely at the Jewish Christian gospels. We will need to ask: Where did these gospels come from? Who wrote them? How are they different? And how significant are the differences? By far the most important question to ask is: How do we know whether the Jewish gospels were more historically *reliable* at introducing us to Jesus than the four biblical ones?

Which Gospels are reliable?

In trying to sort this out we run into something that many Muslims and Christians are unaware of: Christianity and Islam are largely in the very same boat when it comes to working out whether their sacred historical texts are reliable. This is especially true in the case of the *Gospels* and the *hadith*. Whatever their differences, both sorts of text bear extraordinary similarities in pure historical terms:

- They are both reports of the life events and teaching of a divine prophet.
- They both rely on eye-witness testimony to those events and teachings.

- They both rely on the reliability of those eye-witnesses.
- They both circulated in a community of followers.
- They both existed in oral form before they were committed to paper.
- They were both written down well after the prophet's death.
- They were both passed along a chain of testimony.
- In both cases, many of their reports rely on multiple witnesses and multiple accounts.
- In both cases, we can recognize interlocking chains of testimony.

Now, this isn't simply an interesting quirk of history. It is important. It means that Muslims and Christians (should) agree on how to evaluate the historicity of their eye-witness testimonies. Indeed, as it happens, the method developed within Islam to evaluate the reliability of the *hadith* is eminently suitable for evaluating the reliability of the eye-witness account of Jesus' life.

So how did Muslim scholars determine which hadith were authentic? By assessing a) the quality of the report, b) the quality of the reporters, and c) the quality of the transmission of the report. They asked lots of sensible questions like:

- How close to the events was the original report? Was the report made by an eye-witness? Or was the report hearsay?
- Was the eye-witness an authority? Did he know Muhammad personally? Was he a trusted leader in the community?
- Was this eye-witness reliable? Was he of good character? Did he have a good memory? Was he trusted as a reporter?
- How well was the report passed along? Was the chain of testimony a long one? Were there any gaps in the chain: where one or more of the transmitters is missing from the records?
- Was the event reported on by more than one witness? Are the chains overlapping: i.e. do they share common reporters?
- Does the content of the report make sense? Is it the sort of thing Muhammad would be likely to do? Is it consistent with Islamic teaching and practice?

In short, this hadith science carefully examined both the content of any report (the *matn*), and its transmission process (the *isnad*).

How do the Gospel of the Hebrews, and the four biblical Gospels, negotiate these sorts of questions?

The Gospel of the Hebrews

What do we know about the Gospel of the Hebrews? As it happens *extremely* little. Ancient Christians mentioned three Jewish gospels – the Gospel of the Hebrews, The Gospel of the Nazarenes, The Gospel of the Ebionites – but we have very little clue about what any of these texts contained. Indeed, it is not even clear whether they were three different gospels, or three names for the same text. The reason we are in the dark about this is because there are no existing Jewish gospels! We have no original texts, no copies of the texts, and no fragments of the texts. All we know of their content is found in a few brief quotations by early Christian scholars.

Just how ignorant we are about the Gospel of the Hebrews is exposed when we start to ask hadith science questions: Who is the author of this gospel? We don't know. Where was this gospel written? We don't know that either. Who held the authoritative text? We have no idea. How was it transmitted? We simply don't know. When was it written? Again, we don't know, but since it was being quoted in the late second century CE, most scholars guess sometime in the early second century. What language was it written in? We don't know, but probably Hebrew.

Was its content religiously acceptable? Since we have so little of the text available this is hard to say. However, from the few quotes we do have, probably not – at least not for orthodox Muslims or Christians. Muslims will likely find it problematic since it affirms Jesus' resurrection from the dead. Listen:

> And when the Lord had given the linen cloth to the servant of the priest, he went to James and appeared to him. For James had sworn that he would not eat bread from that hour in which

he had drunk the cup of the Lord until he should see him risen from among them that sleep. And shortly thereafter the Lord said: Bring a table and bread! And immediately it is added: He took the bread, blessed it and brake it and gave it to James the Just and said to him: My brother, eat thy bread, for the Son of man is risen from among them that sleep. (Jerome, *De viris inlustribus* 2)[49]

Christians will probably be unhappy with it too. Its description of the relationship between Jesus and the Holy Spirit is unorthodox at best. Jesus is recorded as saying:

Even so did my mother, the Holy Spirit, take me by one of my hairs and carry me away on to the great mountain Tabor. (Origen, *Commentary on John*)[50]

Now, this is all deeply dissatisfying in terms of establishing the place of the Gospel of Hebrews in the Muslim Jesus conspiracy. In hadith science terms, we have no *isnad* and a dodgy *matn*: we have no sense of the reliability of the text and the very little we know of the content is suspect. The Gospel of the Hebrews fails to pass muster by Muslim historical standards. If it were a *hadith* it would have been thrown out long ago. Why would anyone use it as evidence for a conspiracy?

The only possible way the conspiracy can jump this hurdle is if there is solid evidence that the Gospel of the Hebrews was deliberately destroyed and written out of history, then replaced by false gospels. Is there any evidence for this? None whatsoever. Unsurprisingly then, no supporters of the theory points to any.

The four Gospels

Still, it is possible that the biblical Gospels are unreliable too. Earlier I told the story of how the Bible came to have four Gospels. How does this story stand scrutiny by the standards of hadith science? As it happens, much better. For a start, we can identify the authors and contexts of each Gospel. There is, though, so much more to say about the historicity of these texts. Here's just a few important things.

First, the biblical Gospels are the *oldest* gospels in existence. Almost all scholars date them late in the first century: Mark as early as 70 CE, Matthew and Luke between 80–90 CE and John perhaps as late as 100 CE. These dates are uncontroversial among professional historians – and they are critical for historical reliability. It means that the Gospels are records of high-quality eye-witness testimony. It means the authors were witnesses to the events (or their scribes) and were trusted leaders of the first Christian communities. And, it means that very many other eye-witnesses to Jesus' life were still alive – and that they could have kicked up a stink if the story was concocted. It means, too, that historians unquestionably treat these Gospels as the most reliable historical windows into Jesus' life on earth.

Second, the fact there were *four* Gospels is a great thing for the sake of reliability. It means there were multiple, confirming testimonies to the events of Jesus life. The fact they shared some source material (the so-called Q) is not a problem here. It simply reinforces that, like the *hadith*, all four Gospels were produced in community. They exhibit four different takes on what was a shared experience of walking with Jesus.

Third, the biblical Gospels display strong and overlapping dissemination patterns. A diagram of just how interlocking the process was is shown on page 70.

This pattern of copying and dissemination meant that, aside from accidental scribal errors, there was virtually no chance of deliberate corruption. It was simply impossible to change, destroy, or influence the message. The gospel cat, so to speak, was out of the bag! As a result, the ancient world has passed down literally thousands of copies of essentially unchanged copies of the Gospels.

If I'm correct about all this, then the last remaining thread of the Muslim Jesus conspiracy theory – at least as outlined – has been cut. Put simply, there is no strong suspect left to pin responsibility for corruption upon; there is no good reason to think that Jewish

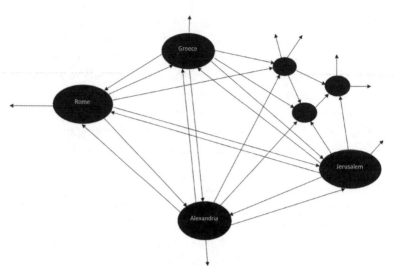

Figure 1 **Gospel dissemination diagram**

Christianity was the true, original Christianity; and there is every reason to treat the four biblical Gospels as both essentially uncorrupted, and the most reliable witnesses available to the Jesus of history. Instead of hard evidence, we have (at best) been presented with mere speculation and highly questionable possibilities. Absent a better theory, it seems extremely unlikely that the Muslim Jesus was preached in a historical line through Abraham, James, the Ebionites and then Muhammad. Where, then, did he come from?

13

The historical Muslim Jesus

All the ancient witness available to us points to the conclusion that the Muslim Jesus is not the Jesus of an original, true, remnant, Jewish Christianity. But – and it's a big but – that doesn't mean that he isn't the Jesus of some sort of ancient Christianity. In fact, he almost certainly is! What the evidence does point to is that the Muslim Jesus is directly related to the Jesus of popular, oral, Arabian tradition.

It is uncontroversial that various oral traditions concerning the Christian Jesus were swirling around Arabia at the emergence of Islam. Griffith explains that:

> stories of the Biblical patriarchs and prophets, and of Jesus the Messiah too, also circulated among those who the Qur'an calls 'Scripture people' … in nonbiblical, noncanonical, literature, in midrashic retellings, in commentaries, in various other Jewish and Christian texts, in rabbinical works such as the Talmuds and in Christian homilies. The latter in particular, in the form of Syriac *memre*, verse homilies, were numerous and widespread at the time of the Qur'an's origins.[51]

Unlike the Gospel of Hebrews, copies of many of the texts these traditions were based upon exist, so we can say with certainty what they contained.

It is plain, too, that the Muslim Jesus tradition aligns *extraordinarily* closely with these earlier oral traditions. Especially regarding the birth, infancy and miracle stories Khalidi recognizes that:

> there is little reason to question their close affinity with certain apocryphal gospels and with Syriac, Coptic and Ethiopic literature.[52]

Indeed, many Muslims and Christians would be surprised to know just how closely aligned to the oral tradition the Qur'an is. Recent scholarship on the Qur'an has revealed that whenever it is outlining a biblical story it does so using *oral formulae*.[53] Oral formulae are patterns or devices used in spoken cultures to help memorize important stories. Remnants of such devices in contemporary English include phrases like: 'Once upon a time', or '…and they all lived happily ever after'. It turns out that more than one quarter of the Qur'an displays just such long formulaic patterns. The reason the Muslim Jesus so neatly aligns with previous traditions is because the Qur'an was simply retelling these earlier traditions using familiar formulae – albeit adapting them to its own style and purposes.

Now, it is true of course that the Muslim Jesus did not resemble the Christian Jesus in every respect. There were aspects of how Christians spoke and thought about Jesus that were anathema to the Qur'an. But there is something interesting going on here: wherever we find significant difference between the Muslim Jesus and the Christian Jesus it is always due to Islam cleansing Jesus of some feature – it is never due to Islam teaching us something new about Jesus life. Of course, it is true that some later traditions sought to add rich detail to Jesus' birth story, and his role in judgement day, but neither of these are new ideas or stories about Jesus. Both are merely embellishments to existing Christian stories. Embellishments aside, Islamic tradition simply seeks to take away what it sees as offensive, rather than add anything new.

What this means is that Islam does not offer us any insight into the historical Jesus that is *independent* of earlier Christian tradition. Islam seems to have no privileged knowledge, no original stories, no special insights and no record of any unique teaching concerning this extraordinary figure. The Qur'anic/traditional Jesus is essentially derivative from the Arab Christian one; the Sufi Jesus is ahistorical with no place and no story; and Akyol's Muslim Jesus has no independent substance. In sheer historical terms, then, the Muslim Jesus brings nothing to the table.

Of course, I'm not the first to have noticed this. Muslims have variously sought to explain it. Khalidi's explanation is novel. He claims that instead of being directly co-opted from Christianity '...the Jesus of the Qur'an is a trustee of an inheritance but not a relative of the testator.'[54] It is hard to know what to make of this idea – it's hard to even know what he means! Apparently, he wants Islam to inherit Jesus from Christianity, without conceding it is a direct relative. Mmmmm. I'm not sure that's how inheritance works. He seems to want to have his cake and eat it too.

Akyol wants to argue for something similar. He believes that the Qur'an, at least, derived its knowledge of Jesus entirely independently of history. Any similarity between the Muslim and Christian Jesuses is due simply to parallel revelatory streams. Putting on his historian's hat, he concedes that this vision of Jesus is ultimately grounded in his faith commitments. Before he even looks at the ancient evidence, his commitment to the Qur'an being the Word of God, and to the unacceptability of a Trinitarian conception of God, render the Christian Jesus necessarily false - and demand some sort of conspiracy theory be true. If this is the case, then he will need to return to the drawing board to develop a new corruption account that will stand historical scrutiny. Until he does so the Muslim Jesus remains an idea, a belief, a person of faith – and not a person who obviously walked this earth to be encountered by real people.

All this calls us to face up to what may be, for some, an uncomfortable reality: the Muslim Jesus appears to have emerged out of religious conviction, not out of the pages of history. Perhaps Muslims won't mind if this is the case. I'm sure the average Muslim will trust the Qur'an over historians every day of the week. I foresee one slight problem with this, though. I'm not sure the Muslim Jesus is any more at home in the Islamic religion than he is in history.

Part 3

LOCATING JESUS

For many years I lived and worked with Somali refugees. They were very recent arrivals, fleeing the civil war that wracked their country well into this century. Upon arrival, many slotted straight into the Australian way of life. Like many Aussies, Somalis have an irreverent sense of humour and an uncomplicated straight-shooting approach to life. Some, however – most commonly the older adults – struggled to come to terms with living in a new place. Usually this was because they still regarded Somalia as home. Since they had been forced to leave, they viewed themselves not as migrants seeking a permanent home, but as 'displaced' people seeking a temporary refuge. This meant that their families, houses, businesses, religious communities, dreams, and purposes were somewhere else. Despite this, being in Australia meant they were forced to modify their behavior. They had to do their family, politics, society, and religion differently. Because of all this, they remained uncomfortable, unsettled. They never properly fitted in since they were 'built' for somewhere else.

My suspicion is that something similar is going on with the Muslim Jesus. While Jesus initially appears as a beautiful figure in Islam, on closer examination he is not really at home. Islam, it seems to me, is not the natural religious habitat of the Messiah. Instead, the Muslim Jesus bears a whole range of religious identity markers that place him as a citizen of traditional Christianity.

14

Place of birth

The most celebrated feature of the Muslim Jesus is his birth. It was soaked in divine activity. It was foreshadowed with prophetic portent. Such strange and wonderful prophecies surrounded his grandfather Imran, and his mother Mary, that these two are rewarded with chapters of the Qur'an being named after them. His birth was made possible by a uniquely miraculous conception by a virgin. No other prophet of Islam – indeed no other human since Adam – was conceived without a human father. Within Islam, Jesus' birth is without precedent and beyond compare – it is truly *extra*-ordinary. I'm wondering why it's there.

Is there any Islamic religious reason why Jesus, alone among all prophets, should have been born of a virgin? There doesn't seem to be. There seems no religious requirement for *any* prophet to be miraculously born – even as a special case. An ordinary birth seemed to be no impediment to any other prophet fulfilling their roles. Indeed, Muhammad – the Prophet of Islam *par excellence* – was born conventionally. Moreover, the Muslim Jesus doesn't seem to have derived any ongoing benefit from his supernatural origins: it doesn't seem to have provided him with any inherent qualities that enhanced his prophetic ministry. So, again, why?

One possible answer is that it was simply God's will and pleasure for things to be this way. In Islam, God is, of course, free to act in extraordinary ways. Sure, this is possible. There is nothing in the account of Jesus' birth that necessarily *contradicts* Islamic doctrine. Muslim scholars, though, usually argue there is more going on here than just that. They point to the events of the virgin birth as a 'sign' of God's reality and power given to the Jews. This is reasonable. It is certainly an Islamic way of operating: the

God of the Qur'an is the God who is all-powerful and regularly provides signs.

But we can still ask: Why *this* sign? Why *this* unique miracle? Why not a different sort of miracle to impress the Jews? Wouldn't it be better for God to have provided a miracle that carried inherent religious meaning? Why not a miracle like, say, the Qur'an – a miracle of prophecy that confirms Muhammad's prophetic status? At best, Jesus' virgin birth seems Islamically *ad hoc*. The Muslim Jesus' virgin birth looks even more random when we compare it to that of the Christian Jesus.

There are, for our purposes, no substantial differences between Islam and Christianity in the 'whats' of the virgin birth. The accounts in the two faiths vary a little in the historical details – for example, in Islam Mary gives birth under a palm tree, whereas in Christianity she does so in the town of Bethlehem – but they agree on the important things. In short, both faiths testify that two thousand or so years ago, in Israel, a religiously faithful young Jewish virgin was blessed with a divinely conceived child, all in fulfilment of a prophetic promise.

There are, however, very substantial differences in the 'whys' of the virgin birth: in Christianity the Messiah must be virgin-born. We can see why in the Gospel of Luke's account of an angelic message announcing Jesus' arrival to the Jews:

> Today in the town of David a Saviour has been born to you; he is the Messiah, the Lord. (Luke 2.11)

Christianity claims Jesus' birth is extraordinary because it is the birth not simply of a prophet, but of a *Saviour*. This child is extraordinary because he will save humanity from their sin, their brokenness, their religious failures.

Christianity understands that for the Saviour to do this remarkable work he needs two key qualifications: 1) he must be human, and 2) he must be sinless. He must be human so that he can properly represent humanity. At the same time, he must be sinless, so he is not bound up in the problem – if he was an ordinary, sinful person he would need rescuing too! Jesus' virgin birth allows both these qualifications to be met. He is properly born human, but from an entirely new line of humanity.

Of course, this understanding is unacceptable to traditional Islam. Indeed, it is viewed as nonsense. Elsewhere I've argued how this Christian account can make philosophical sense in a way that negotiates these sorts of objections, but that is another conversation.[55] My simple point here is that understanding the virgin birth within a Christian framework fills it with rich religious meaning – and in a way that is absent in Islam. The newborn Jesus rests comfortably at home in his cradle in Bethlehem – rather than under his Islamic palm tree – because only Christianity makes sense of a virgin-born Messiah.

The same can be said of how comfortably this baby would bear his names.

15
Names

Names matter. They identify us. They place us in a family, a tribe, a culture, in history. They reveal our family's values or aspirations for us. All my children's names are loaded with meaning: Samuel means 'God hears'; Timothy means 'honouring God'; Nathaniel is named after the biblical Nathaniel – a man without guile; and Jeremy means 'exalted by God'. The Muslim Jesus bears many names. What do they say about him? What religious meaning do they carry? Who do they identify him as?

In the Qur'an, the Muslim Jesus is most commonly referred to as 'the Son of Mary'. This makes sense. It is both properly Arab, and properly Islamic, to locate someone in their family and tribe. Jesus, however, is further identified by honorific titles. Uniquely among the prophets of Islam he is designated as: the 'Messiah', the 'Word of God', and a 'Spirit from God'. Here we are confronted with a similar conundrum we encountered with the virgin birth. How do we fit these titles within an Islamic religious framework? Like the virgin birth, the designation of these titles to Jesus is religiously unprecedented; unlike the virgin birth, each of these titles appear to carry deep and inherent religious meaning.

Word and spirit

In the Qur'an, a prophet's job is simply that of a messenger. Indeed, Islam is at pains to explain that a prophet brings virtually nothing of himself to the communication process. Like a megaphone, he simply passes along the (miraculously) received Word of God to his audience. The essence of the role is to take nothing away from the purity of the divine message by adding any human contribution.

If this is the case, then it seems strange that the prophet Jesus is described as the 'Word of God' and a 'Spirit from God'. These additional qualifications suggest a more profound role as divine representative. They appear to shift Jesus' identity from *speaking* the word of God, to *being* the Word of God; from receiving revelation from its source, *ruh al-Qudus* (the Holy Spirit), to *being* that source. Obviously, traditional Islam can't accept either. What do these names mean?

The traditional explanation is that these two terms are allusions to his virgin birth. So, Jesus is called the Word of God because, like Adam, he was produced not by human means, but by divine command. In the same way, Jesus is called a Spirit from God because, like Adam, he was brought to life through the direct action of God putting breath in his lungs. If this is correct then the titles Word of God, and Spirit from God are simply different ways of saying that, despite being virgin-born, Jesus is merely human.

This explanation is plausible. But, if this is true, then not only is Jesus virgin-born, but he is special in the sorts of ways that Adam was special. This doesn't explain the Jesus anomaly. In fact, instead of normalizing Jesus, it makes him even more extraordinary! Again, why does a 'new Adam' appear on the scene? Islam seems to have no need for one. It is religiously unexpected, unnecessary, and unexplained.

Not so in Christianity. There, it is expected – indeed necessary – that Jesus comes as the new Adam. We see this explained in chapter five of the Book of Romans. Here's a key verse:

> For if many died through one man's trespass, much more have
> the grace of God and the free gift by the grace of that one man,
> Jesus Christ, abounded for many. (Romans 5.15)

This verse is part of a detailed argument. Here it is in a nutshell: Sin entered the world through Adam, the first man, and all humanity was corrupted. This corruption was so profound, so deep, that humanity needed a totally new start. Jesus came as a new Adam to provide that new beginning for any who accept his gift of a new

Spirit-filled life. We need not concern ourselves with just how this could work. For now, the key point is that, from a Christian view of the world, humanity *needed* a new Adam, and so the radical, unique identity of the Christian Jesus made sense.

I'm aware, of course, that Islam disagrees with both this diagnosis of the human condition, and this solution. Islam teaches that humans haven't fallen this far from our created purposes and that, despite our weaknesses, we can be religiously successful without needing such a drastic solution. But this is exactly my point. From an Islamic view of the world there is absolutely no need whatever for a new Adam. So, why is one there?

Messiah

Calling the Muslim Jesus 'Messiah' is similarly perplexing. The Qur'an is silent on both the meaning of the title and its Islamic significance. Certainly, apart from Jesus, we come across no Muslim Messiahs in the Qur'an, or traditions. Muslim scholars have had to speculate on just how the title should be understood in Islam. Many suggestions have been offered for its meaning including: pure, flat-footed, healer, born covered in oil, and, touched by the angel Gabriel. Most though, recognize, and affirm, its historical usage in both Judaism and Christianity. There Messiah literally means 'anointed one' and refers to the practice of pouring oil over the head of those chosen by God for specific roles. If that was all that being Messiah involved, then it would appear Islamically acceptable. Despite no other prophets of Islam being anointed like this, there seems no religious contradiction in anointing one this way.

The problem, however, is that, over time, the title Messiah came to have a much deeper meaning for Jews and Christians than its literal 'anointed person'. The Jewish prophets used it to refer to an ultimate King of the Jews who would reign forever on a heavenly throne. For the Christians Jesus was this anointed one. Given this, it seems strange that the Qur'an would happily affirm Jesus' messianic identity. Even if it was using the word in its literal sense, why did it ignore the opportunity to correct the Christians' deeply offensive exaltation of Jesus above the role of mere prophet?

This is not all. It gets trickier for Islam. That's because even the Islamic tradition affirms Jesus as fulfilling the richer messianic expectation of Jewish prophecy. Recall that the Muslim historian al-Tabari reported that the events of Jesus' childhood fulfilled a seven-hundred-year-old prophecy by Hosea predicting that the Messiah would come 'out of Egypt' (Hosea 11.1). If this were the only messianic prophecy in the Jewish Scriptures, then there wouldn't be a problem. Unfortunately, however, there are many, many more.

Many Muslims might be unaware just how heavily loaded the Jewish Scripture is with prophecies foreshadowing the arrival of the Messiah. Here are just a few, key, examples:

- The Messiah would be virgin-born (Isaiah 7.14)
- The Messiah would be a descendant of David (2 Samuel 7.12)
- The Messiah would be born in Bethlehem (Micah 5.2)
- The Messiah would be called God's Son (Psalm 2)
- The Messiah would be called Wonderful Counsellor, Mighty God, Prince of Peace (Isaiah 7)
- The Messiah would perform healing miracles (Isaiah 35)
- The Messiah would suffer and serve as the representative of Israel (Isaiah 52, 53)
- The Messiah would be rejected (Psalm 118)
- The Messiah would ride into Jerusalem on a donkey (Zechariah 9.9)
- The Messiah would be betrayed for thirty pieces of silver (Zechariah 11.12)
- The Messiah would be stabbed but vindicated (Psalm 22)
- The Messiah would be resurrected (Psalm 16)
- The Messiah would establish a new covenant with God (Jeremiah 31.31)

There is something important to notice about these prophecies. They are not simply historical predictions that a virgin-born prophet would turn up one day. No. Instead, these are precisely the divine promises that *defined* the title 'Messiah' and shaped Jewish expectations. So, the Jewish scriptures were foreshadowing a virgin-born King, in the royal line of David, who would perform mighty acts of healing before suffering and being killed upon a tree. Death, however, would not hold him down. He would rise from the dead to establish a new relationship for his people with God. Even this, however, is just the bare bones of the story of the Messiah. There is a lot more going on in these prophecies.

One crucial idea is that the Messiah performs a *representative* role: his job is to represent God's people, Israel. So, just like the Israelites escaping Pharaoh, their representative Messiah would be 'called out of Egypt'. Just like Israel, the Messiah would be tested in the desert. Just like Israel, the Messiah would be called to be a faithful son. Just like Israel, the Messiah would be called to be a light to the nations. Just like Israel, the Messiah would be called to suffer in service. Israel had failed in all these things. The Messiah would not. In short, the ancient prophecies spoke of a Messiah – their king – who would step in to represent Israel in finally fulfilling its purpose as a chosen people of God.

All this leaves the Muslim Jesus in a difficult position. Does he want to be the sort of Messiah that fulfils all these Jewish prophecies? I suspect not. If not, on what basis will he choose which are legitimate? Moreover, is there any place for a representative Messiah in Islam? If there is I can't see it. Instead, traditional Islam holds strongly to the idea that each person is solely responsible for fulfilling the divine call to obedience. No one can bear that load for another and no one can send a representative before God. Surely, then, the Muslim Jesus can't be the Messiah of Judaism and Christianity. And if he isn't, then who is he? Why bear that title at all? Without his prophetic background the Messiah is emptied of meaning within Islam. He is there, but unanchored, without root.

Of course, none of this is a problem for the Christian Jesus. He can happily fulfil every Old Testament messianic prophecy. So happily, in fact, that this fulfilment motif frames the narrative of all four Christian Gospels. Matthew's Gospel starts with:

The book of the genealogy of Jesus, Messiah … (Matthew 1.1)

Mark does the same. His opening words are:

The beginning of the gospel of Jesus, Messiah … (Mark 1.1)

John explains the purpose of his Gospel as being that:

These things are written so that you may believe that Jesus is the Messiah… (John 20.31)

Luke's ending summarizes Jesus' role as fulfilling prophecy thus:

Thus it is written, that the Messiah should suffer and on the third day rise from the dead, and that forgiveness and repentance for the forgiveness of sins should be proclaimed in his name to all nations. (Luke 24.46–47)

We could even say that, at their heart, the Christian Gospels are simply biographies of the promised Messiah. So much so that even if these prophecies were all we had – that is, even if we had no Gospels – we could tell the story of Jesus as Messiah: this short list of Old Testament prophecies outline the basic plot of all four biblical Gospels. So much so, incidentally, that suggestions that other Jewish gospels describing Jesus as merely a prophet might be authentic are rendered meaningless.

Jesus' Muslim names unavoidably place him in Christianity, not Islam. This really shouldn't be any surprise – especially if Muslims want to call him Messiah. 'Christ' is simply the Greek word for Messiah, and so Christianity is, and always has been, literally: 'Messianity'. It should go without saying that the Messiah is at home there.

16

Behaviour

The Christian Jesus told this story:

> What do you think? A man had two sons. And he went to the
> first and said, 'Son, go and work in the vineyard today.' And
> he answered, 'I will not,' but afterward he changed his mind
> and went. And he went to the other son and said the same.
> And he answered, 'I go, sir,' but did not go. Which of the two
> did the will of his father? They (Jesus' hearers) said, 'The first.'
> (Matthew 21.30–31)

Here he is recognizing a deep truth: your actions count more than
your words in identifying who you are and where you truly belong.

In Islam, miracles are astonishing actions that truly identify
God's existence and character. They are understood as pointing,
dramatically and evidentially, to things like His power, His
knowledge, His sovereignty or His gracious provision. For a
miracle to operate as a sign then, it can't just be any old amazing
event. Instead, it needs to have inherent religious meaning: the
nature of the miracle needs to point to the nature of God. This is,
prototypically, the case in Islam's greatest miracle – the Qur'an.
Muhammad is a messenger, and so his accompanying sign is a
miraculous message. The sign, then, is deeply Islamic.

The Muslim Jesus' miracles are portrayed as divine signs. So, the
Qur'an records that he spoke while still a baby in order to confirm
his prophetic role and to defend his mother against accusations of
sexual immorality (Q19.30–33). That is sensibly a sign that God
speaks through prophets. Similarly, Jesus is recorded as healing the
blind and the leprous (Q3.49) That, too, is reasonably a sign that God
is powerful and merciful. And again, when Jesus is seen breathing

life into clay birds, and raising the dead – both by God's permission (Q3.49) – these are signs that straightforwardly point to the truth that God is the author of life. All these miracles happily operate as signs pointing to God. But do they fit nicely within Islam?

At best, it is fair to say that Jesus' miracles are Islamically *unusual*. Other than Moses, no other Qur'anic prophet is seen performing these sorts of amazing acts. Not even Muhammad was accompanied by divine accreditation from start to finish of his life. Jesus was miraculously born; Muhammad conventionally. Jesus supernaturally spoke, healed, and gave life; Muhammad only received visions. Jesus was raised directly to heaven; Muhammad died of illness. Why so many signs?

One common Muslim explanation for this anomaly relates to audience. It runs like this: the Jews were a people for whom miracles were an especially suitable proof of divine endorsement, so when the Muslim Jesus was sent as a messenger to the Jews he was provided with miracles. Perhaps. It's certainly possible. Still, this doesn't sit properly with me for one simple reason: the miracles of the Muslim Jesus are just as *unusual in Judaism*. Again, other than a few isolated cases,[56] no Old Testament prophet is seen performing these sorts of amazing acts or being accompanied from start to finish with divine accreditation. If the Jews needed many extraordinary signs before they accepted someone as a prophet, then why were they happy to accept Isaiah and Jeremiah and Ezekiel and Hosea, and all the rest, as prophets?

Whatever the explanation, there's an even bigger problem: the Muslim Jesus performs miracles that endorse things that are *positively denied* by Islam. Earlier we noted Jesus' lone Qur'anic prayer:

> O Allah, our Lord, send down to us a table from heaven to be for us a festival for the first of us and the last of us and a sign from You. And provide for us, and You are the best of providers. (Q5.114)

The story goes that, in answer to this prayer, God miraculously provided a huge table overflowing with food. Some later traditions even suggest it was so laden with provisions that it allowed thousands of people to be fed. At face value, this is an Islamically straightforward story of divine provision: Jesus prays that God would miraculously provide for his disciples; his prayer is answered. The sign on view here seems to be that God is a gracious giver.

There is, however, a lot more going on here than just that. Virtually all scholars understand the Qur'an here to be describing Jesus' last supper with his disciples. Moreover, the festival (*Eid*) referred to in the prayer is almost certainly the Christian communion/eucharist – a ritual meal that operates as a remembrance of that original supper. If this is correct, we are left with a conundrum: How does such a festival fit within Islam?

This is a conundrum because in Christianity the last supper (and the eucharist) is not simply a sign of God's provision of food, but of *salvation*. It refers both *backward* to the Jewish Passover salvation festival, and *forward* to Jesus' saving death. In fact, the biblical last supper describes Jesus reimagining, or reinterpreting, the original Passover meal in light of his own ministry. The Passover was about a sacrifice paying for sin. In the first Passover supper a lamb was sacrificed; in this last Passover supper Jesus would be sacrificed. This doesn't feel very Islamic.

The dilemma is sharper even than that. Recall that this is not the first time we've come across the Muslim Jesus teaching this idea. Al-Tabari reported him saying:

> What I have done with you tonight in serving you the meal, washing your hands with mine – this is to make you and me equal. You consider me the best of you, so do not be arrogant towards one another. Sacrifice yourselves for one another, just as I sacrifice myself for you. My request of you is that you call out to God; call out fervently to postpone my end.[57]

We wondered before what sort of sacrifice was on view here. Now we can see that the report is straightforwardly describing the traditional Christian view. Jesus' sacrifice was *vicarious* – that is, as the report puts it 'for his disciples' or on their behalf.

Once again, we are confronted with a sign – and festival – that Islam seems to have little need, or religious space for. The whole notion of Jesus' sacrificial death is anathema in Islam, and there are no atoning salvation events to celebrate. That's not to say, of course, that Islam has no idea of sacrifice *at all*. It does. During *Eid ul-Adha* a ritual animal sacrifice is offered in remembrance of the time Abraham offered a ritual sacrifice. The type of sacrifice on view in this Islamic *Eid*, however, is one of thanksgiving, not atonement. The Muslim Jesus' table miracle, then, doesn't seem to fit into ordinary Islam.

Speaking Islamically, this looks like yet another missed opportunity! The eucharist (along with baptism) is the most important sign and festival in orthodox Christianity. For two thousand years, week by week, service by service, it has declared Jesus' death on the cross as an atonement for sins. There has *never* been a time when Christians didn't celebrate it in their gatherings. If Christians had gotten all this wrong, wouldn't this prayer have been the perfect opportunity for the Qur'an to correct a horrible misunderstanding? How could the Qur'an offer even a passing nod to a heretical event?

Going back to the key point: what do the Muslim Jesus' actions in this miracle say about his home? For mine, he looks suspiciously like the first son in Jesus' story – saying one thing but doing another. In Islam, Jesus says no to the need for salvation, but then offers a salvation miracle. He says no to atoning sacrifice for sins, but then celebrates an atonement festival. By this (and all his other actions) he is more a son of Christianity than of Islam.

17

Speech

One easy way to work out where someone comes from is to listen to how they talk. Our accents, vocabularies, topics of interest and the concepts we use to express ourselves are all clues to our place of origin. The Muslim Jesus' speech clearly reveals that he is not originally from the Islamic world. The sayings attributed to him in Muslim traditions bear all the hallmarks of him speaking and thinking Christianly. They describe a biblical world, with biblical language and using biblical concepts. He pictures something called 'the Kingdom of God', calls for pursuit of 'salvation', and speaks of God as 'Father'. None of these terms or ideas are found in the Qur'an. Can they easily be welcomed into Islam?

Tarif Khalidi argues that they can. He claims that Jesus' sayings were happily accommodated by Muslim tradition because, despite being drawn from Christian tradition, they properly fitted within a traditional Islamic 'conceptual framework'. I can see why he might think that. At first glance, the speech of the Muslim Jesus appears to simply point people to a profoundly Godward life. Surely any God-fearer could be happy with that. On closer examination though, some of the key concepts Jesus has in mind appear alien to a traditional Muslim religious worldview. Let's take that closer look.

Kingdom

The idea of the Kingdom of God (or Kingdom of Heaven) is central to the Christian Gospels. It describes the ideal situation where the universe flourishes obediently under God's rule. This is seen to be the final goal of all creation and is a core theme in Jesus teaching.

He arrives asking the question: 'With what can we compare the kingdom of God, or what parable shall we use for it?' (Mark 4.30) and proceeds to tell story after story that provide rich insight into just what living in this Kingdom entails.

This language of 'Kingdom', though, is foreign to Islam. The Qur'an never uses the term this way. Of course, that doesn't mean it can't translate across. In Islam, as in Christianity, God is the King of the universe – one of the ninety-nine names of God is *al-Malik* (the King). In Islam, as in Christianity, the goal of creation is flourishing obedience under divine sovereignty. So, any potential translation problem here would not stem from Islam having no space for thinking about the creation as God's realm.

No. Where I see a problem is that when the Christian Jesus speaks about the Kingdom of God, he envisions *himself* as its King. This shouldn't be surprising. We have already seen Jewish expectations were that when the Messiah turned up he would exercise his kingship. And that's exactly what happened. The Gospel of Matthew records John the Baptist announcing Jesus' impending arrival like this:

Repent, for the Kingdom of Heaven is at hand. (Matthew 3.2)

Jesus began his teaching with the bold claim that:

The time is fulfilled, and the Kingdom of God is at hand; repent and believe the gospel. (Mark 1.15)

Later, he makes it perfectly clear that the Kingdom of God is *his*. When challenged as to whether he really is the King of the Jews he answers:

My Kingdom is not of this world. (John 18.36)

Surely this would be hard for traditional Muslims to accept. Surely Jesus even hinting that he shares with God in ruling the universe risks the Islamic sin of *shirk* (association with God). Surely, for the idea of the Kingdom of God to make sense in Islam it must be understood differently to the way the Christian Jesus spoke of it.

Salvation

The way the Christian Jesus thought and spoke about 'salvation is also hard to fit into Islam. I'm not alone in thinking this. The influential American Muslim philosopher Ismail al-Faruqi identified the problem this way:

> ... in the Islamic view, human beings are no more 'fallen' than they are 'saved'. Because they are not 'fallen', they have no need of a saviour. But because they are not 'saved' either, they need to do good works – and do them ethically – which alone will earn them the desired 'salvation'. Indeed, *salvation* is an improper term, since, to need 'salvation', one must be in a predicament beyond the hope of ever escaping it. But [according to Islam] men and women are not in that predicament.[58]

Al-Faruqi is overstating his point – possibly for rhetorical effect. Islam, of course, does have some concept of salvation. The Qur'an regularly impresses upon its hearers the need for humans to escape divine judgement and secure entry into eternal paradise. Several times it repeats an exemplary believers' prayer for God to:

> Forgive those who have repented and followed Your way and protect [lit. save] them from the punishment of Hellfire. (Q40.7; also 2.210, 3.16, 3.191)

Essentially, this is the same salvation – the same escape, and securing – that is on view in Christianity. Faruqi's point is not that Islam has no place for salvation at all, but that its understanding of just what is required for salvation is different from Christianity's. Indeed, radically different.

This Muslim believers' prayer points clearly to how salvation is achieved in Islam. Traditionally four things are required: 1) belief in God/Islam, 2) repentance from disobedience, 3) performance of good works, and 4) divine favour/mercy. There are, of course, different schools of thought in Islam concerning the precise character of each of these four requirements, and how they relate. These need not concern us. The important thing to recognize for this discussion is that, in Islam, salvation is entirely a matter between the individual believer and God. In that regard humans can uphold their responsibilities and so there is no need for a Saviour. Or, perhaps better, in Islam salvation is only found in God's heavenly mercy.

Plainly, this is *not* what the Christian Jesus had in mind when he spoke of salvation. He imagined a very different sort of salvation – and a very different Saviour. He (famously) taught that salvation was not through God simply forgiving (although it is that), but also involved God's action on earth through his Son:

> God did not send his Son into the world to condemn the world, but in order that the world might be saved through him. (John 3.17)

He then clearly declared that he, *himself*, was that Saviour:

> I did not come to judge the world but to save the world. (John 12.47)

All the ancient witnesses agreed: angels announced it at Jesus' birth; God himself testified to it at Jesus baptism; and, John, the closest of Jesus' followers, spoke on behalf of all those early human witnesses when he claimed that:

> we have seen and testify that the Father has sent his Son to be the Saviour of the world (1 John 4.14)

All four ancient, apostolic, Christian communities fully accepted this. That the Christian Jesus presents as Saviour is clear – and clearly un-Islamic.

Father

The Muslim Jesus is happy to call God 'Father'. Perhaps traditional Islam can accommodate this, but I'm not sure how. It has been regularly pointed out that, while Islam describes ninety-nine names for God, none of them is 'Father'. Moreover, the Qur'an seems unhappy with the idea:

> ... the Jews and the Christians say, 'We are the children of Allah and his beloved.' Say, 'Then why does he punish you for your sins?' Rather you are human beings from among whom he has created ... (Q5.18)

To me, this verse points to an inescapable fact: there has, historically, been a stark difference between how Christianity and Islam describe the proper way to approach God.

The traditional schools of Islam conceived of the relationship between God and humans primarily as that of Lord and slave. This sort of relationship is characterized, first and foremost, in terms of obedience. The Lord commands, or expresses, his will; the slave or servant obeys. Interestingly, even Sufi mystics – those traditionally seeking a deeper intimacy with God – do not typically think of intimacy with God in familial terms. Instead, ultimately, they pursue an *impersonal* losing of oneself in God.

Jesus, in contrast, taught that God is essentially personal and, indeed, familial. He is a heavenly Father and humans are his children. Indeed, he taught that *all* humans remain God's beloved children no matter how far they have fallen into disobedience. He explores this relationship in a famous story of a son who, after horribly rejecting and shaming his father, thought to himself:

> I will arise and go to my father, and I will say to him, 'Father, I have sinned against heaven and before you. I am no longer worthy to be called your son. Treat me as one of your hired servants.' And he arose and came to his father. But while he was still a long way off, his father saw him and felt compassion,

and ran and embraced him and kissed him. And the son said to him, 'Father, I have sinned against heaven and before you. I am no longer worthy to be called your son.' But the father said to his servants, 'Bring quickly the best robe, and put it on him, and put a ring on his hand, and shoes on his feet. And bring the fattened calf and kill it and let us eat and celebrate. For this my son was dead, and is alive again; he was lost, and is found.' And they began to celebrate. (Luke 15.18–24)

The metaphorical point here for Jesus is that God, the Father, would suffer any humiliation and shame for the sake of restoring His children to the family.

We can see the stark contrast between these two scriptures: the Qur'an denies the Fatherhood of God and suggests punishment for presuming it; the Gospel affirms it and promises celebration for embracing it. We can see it, too, in the daily prayers of believers: Muslims begin by addressing God as 'Lord of the worlds'; Christians begin with 'Our Father in heaven'. How can Islam be happy with the kind of divine intimacy imagined by Jesus?

What's going on here? If I'm correct that Jesus' ideas about kingdom and salvation and the fatherhood of God are deeply un-Islamic, then how has Islamic tradition happily welcomed his teaching?

My hunch is that Islamic tradition has fallen into the classic cross-cultural mistake of *misunderstanding foreign terms*. It's an easy trap to fall into. It's easy to simply assume someone from a different culture means words the same way you do, and in so doing fail to appreciate their full meaning. It's easy to miss subtleties in translation. It's easy to be ignorant of the full religious imagination of another faith. It's easy to read the scriptures of another faith through your own religious imagination. In cross cultural communication it's so easy – despite all good intentions – to be misheard, misrepresented or misconceived. This is understandable. All any of us can do is think and listen with the concepts available. I remember a friend of mine who first encountered talk of the Christian God while still a Buddhist. The only way his religious background allowed him to imagine God was as a statue of a sitting fat man. Because of this, virtually nothing of what Christians said made any sense to him. How, he wondered, can a statue create or command or judge or answer prayer?

Yet while cross-cultural misunderstandings are understandable, it is, in this case, inexcusable. Islamic tradition has failed to do the work of seeking to understand the Christian Jesus on his own terms. It has neglected (for the most part) even so basic a requirement as examining the scriptures carefully to establish his back story. In so doing, his teaching has been evacuated of its original meaning. Instead of being properly translated, it has been superficially reinterpreted. Instead of being fully welcomed and embraced for all he has to offer, Jesus has suffered the enduring problem of visitors to a foreign land – being frustratingly misunderstood and undervalued.

18
More than he seems ...

In the movie *The Equalizer*, Denzel Washington plays a hardware store man named Robert McCall who presents as a friendly and humble middle-aged man, living a quiet life helping co-workers and customers alike. But McCall is not what he seems. He has a past life as a CIA operative that provides him with the skills to moonlight as a vigilante exercising judgement and punishment upon criminals who avoid the law.

I see echoes of McCall in the Muslim Jesus. In Islam, Jesus presents as a mere prophet. Like all prophets, his essential role is to pass on messages from God – in his case the *injeel*. But Prophet Jesus is not what he seems. Even in his prophetic 'day job' we know he is different to other prophets: he is virgin-born; he works miracles; he bears titles of honour. This, however, is nothing compared to his 'night job'. The most stunning role given to the Muslim Jesus is on judgement day. There, he is the executor of God's judgement, separating the good from the evil, destroying enemies, and welcoming the righteous into paradise.

It is hard to over-emphasize the weight of this. The judgement day is one of the most significant tenets of Islam. It, literally, looms large as one of the core Muslim beliefs and central themes of the Qur'an. It is the horizon that all life on earth is lived under. It is the ultimate revealer of the human heart. It is the gateway into eternal bliss. It is also catastrophic, violent, a battlefield. And at the centre of it all is Jesus.

Recall his role outlined in the Hadith:

and it will be at this very time that Allah will send 'Isa [Jesus], son of Maryam [Mary] who will descend at the white minaret in the eastern side of Damascus, wearing two garments lightly dyed and placing his hands on the wings of two angels. When he will lower his head, there would fall drops of water from his head, and when he will raise it up, drops like pearls would scatter from it. Every disbeliever who will find his (i.e., 'Isa's) smell will die and his smell will reach as far as he will be able to see. He will then search for Dajjal until he will catch hold of him at the gate of Ludd (village near Jerusalem), and will kill him. Then the people, whom Allah will have protected, will come to 'Isa son of Maryam, and he will wipe their faces and will inform them of their ranks in Jannah

On earth the Muslim Jesus is a prophet, but in heaven he is also a warrior and a welcomer. He is the deliverer of divine punishment and the doorman to paradise.

Again, I'm wondering why Jesus gets the job? In this case, though, I don't expect the answer to be obvious. The judgement day is properly shrouded in mystery. Involving, as it does, the inbreaking of eternity, it is an event both outside time and comprehension. Mere humans are simply not in a place to assess its whys and wherefores. Still, we can say one thing for certain. The glimpses Islam offers into this day make it clear that the Muslim Jesus is not merely a messenger. At the very least, this seems unexpected.

Not so in Christianity. There, it seems entirely natural that Jesus would take centre stage on judgement day. Natural because, in Christianity, the Messiah is a warrior King. Natural because, in Christianity, the Messiah sits on the judgement throne of the Kingdom of God. And natural because, in Christianity, alone among men, Jesus forged the way through death and judgement into eternal life. Paul puts it like this:

The times of ignorance God overlooked, but now he commands all people everywhere to repent, because he has fixed a day on which he will judge the world in righteousness by a man whom he has appointed; and of this he has given assurance to all by raising him from the dead. (Acts 17.30–31)

This makes sense. Who else would you expect to meet on the day of resurrection but the first resurrected human – the Messiah?

19
At home

Unquestionably Jesus dwells in Islam. But on what terms? At the risk of trivializing the issue, the image that comes to mind is that the Muslim Jesus wears his Islam like an ill-fitting suit. Let me explain. A generous friend recently gave me an Armani suit as a gift. It is, of course, beautiful. The cut, the material, and the workmanship are all exquisite. I do have one problem with it though. Because it wasn't made for me, it doesn't really fit properly. I can squeeze into it, but not easily. In some places it is too tight a fit; in others too loose. From some angles I look good in it; from others not so good. It is the best you can buy, but I'm not entirely comfortable in it. If all we've seen in the preceding chapters is accurate then something similar is going on with the Muslim Jesus.

However beautiful Islam might be, Jesus doesn't appear to fit comfortably into it. He is different to all other Muslims. He turns up mysteriously, identifies unusually, talks strangely and acts weirdly. Too many of his titles are anachronistic; too many of his words are dislocated from their context; too many of his actions are out of the box. He feels more like a guest or a visitor than a citizen. He is welcomed but struggles to gel with the day to day patterns of his new dwelling. He is accommodated but never quite accepted for who he really is. In short, we have seen that Jesus does not appear to be at home there. He feels *too big* for his Islamic role. Of course, just how much bigger is the key dispute between Christianity and Islam.

Going too far?

Christians say Jesus is as big as God! The Qur'an clearly admonishes them for going too far in this regard: O people of the Scripture, do not commit excess in your religion … (Q4.171) My Muslim friends admonish me the same way. Many times, I've been told that Jesus never said the words: 'I am God'. And, of course, they are correct. But they are only technically correct. The case for Jesus' divinity does not rest on a single claim of Jesus, using those exact words. It is much stronger than that.

To see just how much stronger, we need to recognize that there is so much more to the Christian Jesus than we have seen so far. Where we see the Muslim Jesus through fleeting, incomplete glimpses, we view the Christian Jesus through so many more windows. In Christian scripture and tradition, he goes by so many more names than he is accorded in the Qur'an, performs so many more miracles than are recorded in Muslim history, explains so much more richly the nature of the Kingdom than the Sufi Jesus, fulfils so many more Old Testament prophecies than we've seen, and meets so many more Jewish expectations. Christians are prepared to commit the (admittedly astonishing) 'excess' of worshipping Jesus as Lord because of the cumulative effect of all that these details show about him.

Exploring all this would take its own book. But, briefly, the cumulative case for the divinity of Christ includes that:

- The **names** of the Christian Jesus exalt him far above any prophet. He is called the Messiah, the Word of God, the Son of God, Emmanuel (God with us), Mighty God, Saviour, Redeemer, the King of Kings and the Lord of Lords.
- The **miracles** of the Christian Jesus encompass all the actions of God. He is praised by angels, he glorified by the Holy Spirit, he commands the weather, he provides, he heals, he reveals the content of hearts, he brings the dead to life – indeed, he defeats death itself.
- In his **teaching**, the Christian Jesus equates and identifies himself with God – so much so he is regularly accused of blasphemy. He claims pre-existence like God, prescience like God, honour worthy of God, and the keys to life and death, heaven and hell.

- He fulfils **prophecies** that God would manifest himself in person on earth, and that he would be called God.

All these features cohere stunningly, and climax perfectly, in his death and resurrection. Along the way we've gained glimpses of this. We've seen how Jesus life, death and resurrection fulfils the array of messianic prophecies. We've seen how Jesus' death fulfils the sacrificial system enacted most dramatically in the Passover.

But there's so much more.

If we had more time, we could further see how Jesus fulfils the Prophet Ezekiel's foretelling of a Good Shepherd leading God's people into sanctuary. We could see him fulfilling the prophet Jeremiah's promise of a time when the law will be Spiritually written on people's hearts – and so a legal system of religion will become redundant. We could see how Jesus fulfils the promise made in the Book of Genesis that, one day, a descendant of Adam would finally defeat Satan. We could go on to see how Jesus accepted the worship accorded to God; how he was honoured in the way God is honoured; and how God himself spoke from heaven as a witness on his behalf.

Sure, Jesus may not have uttered the exact phrase 'I am God', but every name, every fulfilled prophecy, every miracle, every kingdom story cried it out. One biblical scholar put it like this:

> The case for the deity of Christ does not rest on a few proof-texts. The popular notion that some fourth-century Christians decided to impose on the church a belief in Jesus as God and wrenched isolated Bible verses from their contexts to support their agenda is a gross misrepresentation of the facts. The framers of the orthodox doctrines of the Incarnation and the Trinity did have an agenda, but it was not to replace a merely human Jesus with a divine Christ. Their agenda was to safeguard the New Testament's clear teaching of the deity of the Lord Jesus Christ.[59]

I imagine all this to operate like rope. Ropes are made from tiny fibres of cotton. Individually these fibres have little strength.

However, when intertwined they have the strength to pull supertankers. Similarly, the case for Jesus divinity is intertwined in thread after biblical thread.

At home?

My house is at the edge of the city, close to the bush, and so we are visited by many parrots. A few months ago, a spectacular new parrot appeared on our verandah. A little research revealed it was a Superb Parrot. Despite being a beautiful addition, it turned out the Superb parrot didn't belong. It was hundreds of kilometres out of its territory. Why was it there? Possibly it was an escaped pet. Possibly it was ranging far and wide due to its home habitat being degraded. Whatever the reason, it didn't really belong. It wasn't properly at home – and so it soon moved on.

To me, this well illustrates the religious situation of the Muslim Jesus. In Islam, he is an extraordinary discovery, but he doesn't feel properly located there. He seems dislocated from his natural 'messianic' habitat. That habitat is Christianity. There, his origins fit, his miracles belong, his teaching coheres, and he makes sense of Jewish prophecy. This is true even if we only accept the accounts of these things we find in Muslim tradition. In the end, in Islam, Jesus is striking, but dislocated. In Christianity, he is glorious, and religiously at home.

Part 4

FOLLOWING JESUS

20

Common roads?

Muslims and Christians disagree profoundly about Jesus. Everything we've seen so far confirms it. We disagree about who he is, his place in history and where he fits in religion. We can't get around the fact that this disagreement is substantial, complex and apparently intransigent. It rests not only on the grounds covered in the previous chapters, but also on various metaphysical and psychological commitments at the core of both faiths. It is the type of debate that resists resolution in spite of many conversations, ponderings, reconsiderings and re-readings.

My experience is that many Muslims find this disagreement frustrating. It seems (to me) that they believe Christians and Muslims *should* agree more than we do, and they can't quite get why Christians don't feel the same way. My hunch is that much of this frustration stems from the fact that Muslims imagine Islam and Christianity to be very much the *same sort of religion*. By this I don't mean that they are both monotheistic religions who believe in a divine creator. No, it's much more 'samey' than that. Traditional Muslims believe that Islam and Christianity stand firmly in the same 'Abrahamic' family of religions that began with Judaism. Indeed, they even think that Islam fulfils or completes the divine story played out through Abrahamic religious history.

In this understanding, Islam and Christianity straightforwardly display all the same sorts of religious features. So, they are both established and sustained through prophetic revelation; they both see humans as responsible moral agents operating within a divine order and under a divine Law; they both call humans to ultimate account for their moral behavior; and, they both see this judgement having eternal consequences. In this way of thinking, Muslims and Christians hold a common vision of the religious life. It is one where humans are (most fundamentally) worshippers who prime responsibility is obedience to God and his Law, and this Law is (most fundamentally) a call to first love God, then to second love your neighbour. So, Muslims see the successful religious person as one who properly fulfils this Law: keeping the Law well (enough) leads to eternal reward, failing to keep the Law well enough leads to eternal punishment.

That this is the case seems as obvious as the nose on my face to the average Muslim. So, they think things like: Surely Christians should agree with this shouldn't they? Didn't Jesus teach it plainly? Wasn't he the first prophet to summarize the religious life in exactly those terms? When he was asked, 'Teacher, which is the greatest commandment in the Law?', didn't he reply, '"Love the Lord your God with all your heart and with all your soul and with all your mind." This is the first and greatest commandment. And the second is like it: "Love your neighbour as yourself." All the Law and the Prophets hang on these two commandments.' (Matthew 22.36–40)? Surely, whatever squabbles Christians and Muslims engage in over detailed doctrine don't negate the simple truth that, at heart, they are walking the same religious road of obedience to divine law, do they?

That this is the popular view was shown by my friend Abdi's 'I love Jesus' T-shirt. Recall the slogan:

I LOVE JESUS
BECAUSE I AM A MUSLIM
AND HE WAS TOO!

What's the mindset here? It's that Muslims love Jesus because he was Muslim – that is, that he walked and talked essentially the same religion as Islam.

That this is also the scholarly view is shown by the recent 'Common Word' document. It consists of an open letter from eminent Muslim leaders to eminent Christian leaders that appealed for both worldwide communities to live peaceably with each other. On what grounds? The grounds that they fundamentally agree on a vision of the religious life that places love of God and neighbour as supreme. So, it opens with this summary statement:

Muslims and Christians together make up well over half of the world's population. Without peace and justice between these two religious communities, there can be no meaningful peace in the world. The future of the world depends on peace between Muslims and Christians.

The basis for this peace and understanding already exists. It is part of the very foundational principles of both faiths: love of the One God, and love of the neighbour. These principles are found over and over again in the sacred texts of Islam and Christianity. The Unity of God, the necessity of love for Him, and the necessity of love of the neighbour is thus the common ground between Islam and Christianity. The following are only a few examples:

Of God's Unity, God says in the Holy Qur'an: Say: *He is God, the One! / God, the Self-Sufficient Besought of all!* (*Al-Ikhlas*, 112.1–2). Of the necessity of love for God, God says in the Holy Qur'an: *So invoke the Name of thy Lord and devote thyself to Him with a complete devotion* (*Al-Muzzammil*, 73.8). Of the necessity of love for the neighbour, the Prophet Muhammad said: '*None of you has faith until you love for your neighbour what you love for yourself.*'

In the New Testament, Jesus Christ said: '*Hear, O Israel, the Lord our God, the Lord is One. / And you shall love the Lord your God with all your heart, with all your soul, with all your mind, and with all your strength.*' *This is the first commandment. / And the second, like it, is this: 'You shall love your neighbour as yourself.*' *There is no other commandment greater than these.* (Mark 12.29–31)

The point? We should live at peace. The reason? Because we basically follow the same religion: Islam and Christianity are founded on exactly the same principles of obedience to the necessary law of love for God and neighbour; and, Muslims and Christians follow exactly the same religious ethic of worship and grace.

Now, if this is correct, then of course disagreements over Jesus are going to be annoying to Muslims. It is easy to imagine my Muslim friends saying: 'Okay, maybe we don't agree on the historical details of Jesus' life, or your worship of him, but since he was basically teaching the same type of religious ethic as Islam can't we just get on with living it out?'

Mustafa Akyol says almost exactly that in his discussion of the Muslim Jesus:

> As Muslims, who are latecomers to this scene, we have disagreements with both Jews and Christians. But we have major agreements as well. With Jews, we agree a lot on God. With Christians, we agree that Jesus was born of a virgin, that he was the Messiah, and that he is the Word of God. Surely, we do not worship Jesus, like Christians do. Yet still, we can follow him. In fact, given our grim malaise and his shining wisdom, we need to follow him.[60]

Again, and in a nutshell, the idea is that, whatever our disagreements, we live in the same religious 'scene' and can agree on his 'shining wisdom' while walking our common road of obedient worship and grace. This sounds appealing. It all seems to make sense. And it does – to Muslims.

This way of thinking, however, doesn't sit well with Christians. Why? Because Christians *don't* agree that Islam and Christianity are basically the same sort of religion, and they *don't* agree that Islam and Christianity share a common vision of the successful religious life. In the Islamic mindset, the Muslim and Christian Jesuses are walking the same religious road; but in the Christian mindset they are walking in the same direction, but along profoundly different routes.

Appreciating this more foundational disagreement about religion is crucial to understanding why the disagreement about

Jesus is so perplexing. And because Jesus did summarize the Law as love of God and neighbour, it will take some work to appreciate the religious difference. To fully grasp it, we will need to walk a little way in the steps of both the Muslim and Christian Jesus.

21

The virtuous path of the Muslim Jesus

As a child I used to play a game called 'Follow the Leader'. As the name suggests, it involves a group of kids copying the actions of a person up the front. Whoever follows the leader's actions accurately stays 'in' the game; whoever fails to follow is thrown 'out'. Since it is a kid's game the leader might cut the followers some slack: they might get a few chances to do the actions properly or they might be allowed to follow imperfectly. Still, to be successful in the game you need to follow well. Poor following leads to expulsion. Islam views the religious life a lot like that. There, success comes from properly following the religious teaching about, and example of, obedience to divine Law provided by the prophets. Good following leads to a good life (and paradise); poor following to a bad life (and hell).

As we've seen, Jesus is one of those prophets. As we've also seen, he is a little unusual. In fact, among the prophets described in the Qur'an he is most unusual, and in ways that, quite frankly, make him a hard act to follow. His origin and identity are so extraordinary and supernatural, his ministry so spectacular and miraculous, and his God-given heavenly tasks so unique and superlative, that nowhere is he presented as a model for the average believer. He is also hard to follow because he provides very little guidance or instruction concerning the ordinary, practical, religious life. For the Muslim Jesus to function as a spiritual guide, then, we will need to rely on his example and teaching in the *Qisas al-Anbiya* – that is, the sayings of the Sufi Jesus we met earlier. The way of life modelled and taught by *this* Jesus is deeply and profoundly good.

Loving God

The most striking thing about the road walked by the Muslim Jesus is that it leads directly and uncompromisingly *toward God*. Over and over, he exhibits an extraordinarily strong ascetic predilection for abandoning any worldly affections that compete with this heavenly focus. So, we find this:

> Jesus once lay his head to rest upon a stone. Satan passed by and said, 'So, then, Jesus, I see you have found something to desire in the world after all!' Jesus picked up the stone from under his head and flinging it at him said: 'Take this, and the world with it!'[61]

Doubtless this saying is hyperbolic: Jesus is exaggerating to make a point. And that point is that, for the obedient religious person, God is at the centre of all things. The love of God is so much the primary obligation of humans that all else pales in comparison. The properly religious need cling to the eternal, and not the passing. They must ascribe the greatest worth to the creator, and not the created. Success in the religious life involves resisting the temptations of the Devil to diminish this focus through worldly attachments.

This is just the life modelled by the Muslim Jesus. He is a man with no family, no trade, no possessions, no investments and – aside from some religious disciples – no earthly entanglements. Instead, his life centres on spiritual disciplines like preaching, fasting and prayer. Unquestionably, he keeps he greatest commandment to love God.

Loving neighbours

The Muslim Jesus, however, also keeps the second commandment: he loves his neighbour too. He is not so otherworldly as to ignore the earthly responsibilities of the religious human. And it is here we see the true appeal of the Islamic prophet Jesus: his call to virtuous living. This call was laid out in his many sayings – some of which we saw earlier. Within Islam, these are called '*adab*' sayings, which roughly equates to the English word 'manners.' An approach to social ethics that arose largely within Indo-Persian Islam, *adab* is best understood as a form of virtue ethic. Virtue ethics is an approach to the religious life which focuses on the cultivation of various virtues or character traits – rather than prioritizing obedience to rules (duty ethics) or seeking good ends (consequentialist ethics). In short, *adab* is fundamentally about *being* a good person.

The Muslim Jesus recognized that being that good person involved cultivating a wide range of social virtues. So, he prioritized service over being served to the point where he would both prepare food for his disciples and then wait on them, this being offered as an example of how to treat the poor. When asked to describe the greatest of all human works he named contentment with God. He denounced impatience with the ignorant; strength without restraint; and, worship characterized by pride before God. He called for the love of neighbour. He warned against entertaining lust by repeatedly glancing at women. He praised gentleness as foundational, generosity as life-giving, and mercy as appropriate for all – both good and evil. He threatened the loss of angelic protection for turning away a beggar with nothing. He declared cruelty to be the worst of all the afflictions of the heart.

At other times, the Muslim Jesus resorted to moral tales, or parables, to tease out these virtues further. Prominent among them is a long tale describing Jesus passing through the Valley of Resurrection. There he encounters a skull who described seven torments of hell reserved for those who: unjustly consume the wealth of orphans, drink wine, libel married women, fail to perform prayer, adorn themselves for other than their spouses, and the lost sinners. Another describes Jesus meeting Satan who is selling various vices to those most susceptible: oppression to kings; pride to nobles; envy to religious scholars; dishonesty to traders; and guile to women.

Surprisingly (to us moderns) the Muslim Jesus saw frivolity as a vice. Upon finding his followers laughing he warned that those who fear God avoid laughter. Their excuse that they were only making a joke was viewed dimly – jokes are not suitable for those of 'sound mind'. Unsurprisingly, on the other hand, we discover a saying that closely parallels the so-called 'greatest' commandment of Jesus in the Gospels:

> 'How can a servant be truly pious before God?' Jesus replied, 'The matter is easy. You must truly love God in your heart and work in His service, exerting all your effort and strength, and be merciful toward the people of your race … as you show mercy to yourself.' (Saying 48)

A combined list of virtues commended by the Muslim Jesus – including service, patience, forbearance, contentment, humility, gentleness, honesty, temperance, sobriety, sexual fidelity, justice and mercy – is unquestionably, and formidably, *good*.

Surely, this is a religious road worth aspiring to. Surely, too, even Christians can agree with that, can't they? Perhaps they can if we look closely at the Muslim Jesus' promotion one specific virtue that Christians have, over the years, seen as a distinctive of their faith alone – the love of enemy.

Loving enemies

The Muslim Jesus remained committed to loving his neighbours even if they were his enemies. Unsurprisingly, here, since life is complex, his lessons are complex. Competing values seem to be at play. At the risk of over-simplifying it appears that the *adab* sayings dealing with conflict head in two directions: some sayings promote social separation for the purposes of religious purity and justice; others promote social inclusivity via grace and forgiveness.

Representing the first type we find the Muslim Jesus promoting hatred and anger toward sinners leading to distancing oneself from them. Striking is a tale of Jesus' mother Mary praying curses upon those who sought to deceive her – and God answering her prayers.

If this was all the Muslim Jesus said, there would appear to be little prospect for developing a rich ethic of conciliation or forgiveness when encountering conflict.

Fortunately, there is a second type of conflict ethic described. The Muslim Jesus defines devotion to God as: doing good to those who harm you; forgiving those who have perpetrated evil against you; attending to the sick who ignore you; being kind to the unkind; generous to the untrustworthy; blessing those who insult you; bearing with the impudent; and praying for one's enemies. This Jesus is happy to move towards the sinful – he visited prostitutes for the purpose of healing them – and willing to regard suffering slander as worthy of reward.

This mix of social virtues offers a rich, subtle, and robust framework for handling difficult relationships. It provides avenues for both gracious forgiveness and righteous anger, for gentle passivity and forceful action. Together with the personal character traits described earlier, the Muslim Jesus' teaching subtly melds a supreme Godward-ness with a substantial social ethic. As a religious way of life, it appears good. Indeed, very good.

So, why can't Christians agree that their religious road is the same as this? Well, it's not because they don't aspire to be good, or because they don't agree the love of God and neighbour is at the heart of social ethics. They do. Like Muslims, Christians love virtue ethics. Like Muslims they love the good and aspire to live virtuously. Christians agree with Muslims that this is precisely the road that God's Law prescribes all humans to walk. So, what's the problem?

The problem with the road the Muslim Jesus walks is not that it fails to follow God's law, but whether it is walkable. Sure, the Muslim Jesus embodies a profoundly good religious life, but the big question (Christians ask) is: Who can walk alongside him successfully? Christians, like me, worry that the answer to that question is: no one can.

22

Who can follow
the Muslim Jesus?

A few years back, I was riding my bicycle along a bush track close to my house. As I was coming quickly down a hill I noticed a long, thick, tree branch lying across the track. Since I was on a mountain bike I thought 'No problem – I'll just jump it'. However, as I got close, and too late, I realized that the branch was, in fact, a very large (and very venomous) black snake! As I went to jump it, it reared up, threatening to strike. Fortunately, I missed hitting it, it missed striking me, and I sped on – unscathed except for a racing heartbeat! The road of Muslim Jesus is, I suspect, a bit like this. At first glance, his religious path appears challenging, but surmountable. On closer examination, though, it carries deadly obstacles that might ward off followers. Certainly, Christians will not walk it. In this chapter I hope to explain why. But first, it will help us to ask whether Muslims are any more likely to take this path. I very much doubt it. Why this is helpful is because any Muslim reluctance to follow the Islamic Jesus is for the *opposite* reasons to Christians. Examining these reasons should clarify why Muslims and Christians walk very different religious paths.

Is this road the straight path of Islam?

The most glaring obstacle I see to Muslims following the Islamic Jesus is that his good religious life looks Islamically *inadequate*. This is not because his teaching itself is necessarily un-Islamic. The sort of virtue ethic in view here seems entirely compatible with traditional Muslim thinking. The Indo-Persians were not alone in articulating the Islamic life in virtuous terms. Indeed, there exists a strong tradition of virtue ethics in Islam. Great thinkers like al-Ghazali and al-Farabi dedicated themselves to articulating a so-called 'science' of *akhlaq*, which literally means character or disposition. This discipline (*ilm al-akhlaq*) drew upon an understanding of things like the fundamental religious and moral nature of humanity (*fitrah*), and the goal of unified human society (derived from the doctrine of *tawhid*) to define the character of the human soul and outline methods for cultivating one's character towards virtue. So, the potential roadblock here is not the emphasis on virtue ethics. That is properly Islamic.

No, the obstacle grows out of the almost total disdain of the Muslim Jesus for the law framework of traditional Islam (and originally Judaism). It is striking that in all the sayings credited to the Muslim Jesus he has *nothing* positive to say about the legislative tradition – and everything negative! He is especially scathing towards the traditional religious leaders, generally viewing them as legalistic hypocrites. Earlier we saw him chastising them for displaying an envious character. In another saying, he widens his critique:

> Jesus said to the religious lawyers, 'You sit on the road to the afterlife – but you have neither walked this road to its end, nor allowed anyone else to pass by. Woe to him who is beguiled by you!' (Saying 276)[62]

Was this complaint targeted at specific lawyers in a particular time and place? Perhaps. Nevertheless, the Muslim Jesus remains silent on how to negotiate the specific demands of Sharia law.

Not only that, the Muslim Jesus also fails to display the ritual rhythms and responsibilities of traditional Islam. Aside from an obvious priority to devote himself to prayer, he displays little interest in participating in the Mosque community or fulfilling formal responsibilities to offer zakat (alms), and complete disinterest in a pilgrimage to the *Kaaba*.

Why the silence on law-keeping? There doesn't appear to be any need for it. Must adherence to law lead to legalism and hypocrisy? I can't see why. Surely it is sensible to think that following the formal rituals and rulings of the Sharia should promote an Islamically virtuous life. Indeed, if the scholarly consensus in the Common Word document is correct, then the Sharia can be summed in the two laws of loving God and loving neighbour anyway. Certainly, al-Ghazali thought so. He was perfectly happy to incorporate obedience to the law into his *ilm al-akhlaq*.

This roadblock to following the Muslim Jesus is essentially the same obstacle that Sufism has often come up against: reconciling an ascetic, mystical, religious life with exercising formal obedience to the Sharia. Unless the Muslim Jesus can offer a satisfactory way through this maze, it is hard to imagine him fulfilling all the needs of a model for today's Muslims. In the end, I wonder whether he displays a life that is Islamically comprehensive enough to be worth following.

Perhaps, though, contemporary mainstream Muslims can reimagine their faith in a way that reconciles a virtue ethic with a legislative ethic – the mystical with the traditional. Perhaps. But even if they can, there's an even more significant roadblock to Muslims following Jesus. It is that they already have a supreme ethical model in Muhammad. There's no avoiding that Akyol is not simply arguing that the Muslim Jesus is a good religious model for today's Muslims. No, he's saying much more than that. He's suggesting that the Muslim Jesus is a *much better model than Muhammad* of the religious life in the contemporary Western context. This is how strongly he puts it:

How can Muslims develop religious ideas that may help them move on from their modern crisis? The typical answer is to go back to the Qur'an and the Sunna, the 'example' of the Prophet Muhammad, and to reread them in the light of our times. This answer, of course, cannot be disputed for it refers to the very sources of Islam. But Muslims also need to see that there is something missing here: that we are living in a context very different from the context of the Qur'an and the Prophet Muhammad. These two sources – the divine message and the divinely ordained messenger – established a whole new religion called Islam and brought it to quick victory. We in the twenty-first century, however, are not supposed to establish a whole new religion. Quite the contrary, we are rather living within a religious tradition that has existed for more than fourteen centuries and which is carrying the burden of all that long history. And we are going through internal turmoil exacerbated by external pressure.

In other words, we Muslims are not living in the context of seventh-century Mecca and Medina. We are rather living in the context of first-century Nazareth and Jerusalem. Therefore, we need a 'prophetic example' fit for the first-century drama. We need the method, and the message, of Jesus. Isn't it none other than Jesus, after all, whose very 'return' is promised in our tradition?[63]

The claim here is strong, clear and uncompromising: As a man of his time, Muhammad fails to provide an adequate religious model for all times; we need a prophet more fit for today than Muhammad; we need a better example than Muhammad (a more suitable *Sunna*); we need a more relevant message than Muhammad; and so, we need Jesus.

Is there any way traditional Islam can accept this? I can't see how. Even if we accept (for sake of argument) that there is something unique about the contemporary Western context, how can Muhammad be properly portrayed as (somehow) inadequate – indeed inferior to Jesus? Isn't Muhammad the ultimate prophet? Isn't he the best example of a man who obeyed the divine law to love God and love your neighbour? Isn't his wisdom supremely shining? Isn't his teaching and example fully sufficient for all people, in all times and in all situations? Shouldn't Muhammad's life ooze all the virtues of the Muslim Jesus anyway? Why can't Muhammad provide a religious model that can negotiate any struggle between competing religious visions in the contemporary religious landscape? Surely Islam needs to be able say he can! In short, if a standard Muhammadan model of social ethic is all it's cracked up to be, then why do we need to follow the Muslim Jesus? The vast majority of Muslims would, I suspect, think we don't.

Hopefully, the reader can see the problem. Mainstream Islam is entirely grounded in following the Law – that is, the Sharia. And the Sharia is entirely grounded in the Qur'an and Sunna – that is, the message and example of Muhammad. And the Qur'an and Sunna corrected all that had been distorted, or lost, in Jesus' message – the *Injil*. How, then, can Muslims follow anyone other than Muhammad in living out the requirements of the law? Surely, they can't.

Is this road the narrow way of Jesus?

Christians can't follow the way of the Muslim Jesus either. It's time to understand why.

It's not because Christians think his life is not good. They can easily buy in to the sort of religious virtue ethic promoted by the Islamic Jesus. They agree that love of God and neighbour is at the core of divine Law.

It's also not because the Muslim Jesus' teaching doesn't align closely enough with Christian understanding of what loving God and neighbour looks like. No, his sayings regularly echo, or even quote, the biblical Jesus. Only a few appear jarring to, or problematic for, Christian ethics. One that leaps out for me is his rebuke of joking and laughing – laughter is blessed for the Christian Jesus (Gospel of Luke 6.21). More problematic are those suggesting dealing with 'sinners' by distancing from them, praying for their demise, or even hating them. And if this was all the Muslim Jesus had to say about evil-doers then Christians would likely turn from following him. However, this is not all the Muslim Jesus has to say. There are overwhelmingly more calls to bear with, act graciously toward and even love enemies. This need not make his virtue ethic inconsistent. Handling evil *is* tricky. When confronted by it there are properly times for anger, forbearance, distance, turning the cheek, rebuking, and (to use a biblical phrase) shaking the dust of your feet. Even hatred is appropriate at times – surely God hates evil. All these bearings might properly fit within an ethic of love for the sinner. In sheer ethical terms then, there is little here for Christians to pick at – and much to embrace.

It's also not because Christians feel a need to own Jesus. I am sure there'd be some who on encountering the sayings of the Muslim Jesus would be tempted to bristle, or quibble, over the original sources of these sayings, thinking (or saying!): 'Hang on, this is all taken from our Jesus!' And perhaps they'd be right to think this – Khalidi is happy to accept them as divine truths that Muslims identified in Christian teaching and texts. Perhaps not. Perhaps, as Muslims claim, some are prophetically revealed. Perhaps others are the product of natural human wisdom alone. It matters not. For them to be accepted by either Muslims or Christians they simply need to be recognized as objective moral truths. This can be the case irrespective of just how we came to know them.

No. I foresee Christians choosing a different path because they see the virtuous road of the Muslim Jesus as *unwalkable*. Here, the problem is not seen to be with the road, but with the walkers. Or again, the problem is not with the excellence of Jesus' example, but of the ability of humans to follow it.

Let me illustrate. Growing up in Australia means lots of time on the beach. I remember that as a little kid I would often play a game of trying to match the footsteps of my dad as we walked along the sand. Since my dad was six feet four inches this was virtually impossible – the gaps between his footsteps were just too big! Christians view the human ability to follow divine Law just like that. The Law itself is brilliant. In fact, it's perfect! It codifies the requirements of loving God and neighbour in exquisite beauty and detail – especially in Jesus spectacular teaching. It sets a moral bar that is the proper aspiration, and measuring stick, of all people. The only problem is that the bar is too high for us to leap over. The footsteps involved in walking the road of religious virtue are simply too huge for us to keep up. The good road is too hard for us.

Put more religiously, this is called the doctrine of original sin. It is the historical Christian claim that humans are not simply weak, or misguided or forgetful when it comes to fulfilling God's Law. Instead, sin is seen to be an unavoidable and devastatingly debilitating condition that renders all of us, unaided, as simply unable to be religiously successful.

That humans experience this dilemma is a core Christian tenet. Muslim philosopher Shabbir Akhtar assesses the Christian position on human moral capacity as deeply and sadly tragic. He says that:

> Christianity has famously seen the religious outlook as being a supremely tragic one...Orthodox Islamic thought has always, by contrast, been characterised by its almost total freedom from the tragic instinct...The resolute determination to guard against the temptation to tragedy is Islam's distinctive contribution to religious anthropology.[64]

He puts the Muslim position like this:

> The Islamic position is morally and doctrinally opposed to this proposed external rescue from the plight of sin. We are not innately deviant or crooked or unsound although we are easily misled into temptation. Divine education therefore suffices. We need mentors who can guide us out of our heedlessness.[65]

Again, there is the Muslim position on ethics in a nutshell: We can be good, we just need guidance or reminders.

Now Islam, of course, may be correct about this. Maybe Christianity is way too pessimistic about the prospects of humans doing what God requires. Certainly, we can find myriad instances of ordinary – and extraordinary – acts of community-building love between Muslims and Christians. In terms of the extraordinary, I am reminded of the time when Egyptian Muslims risked their lives by standing arm in arm with their Coptic Christian neighbour around their besieged churches. As for the ordinary, I've lost count of the times I've been on the receiving end of Muslim hospitality.

Christianity, on the other hand, could defend its position in more depth. So, for example, it doesn't claim that humans can't walk an ethical road *at all* unless they are filled with the Holy Spirit. Christianity and Islam at least hold in common that humans were created good and retain a remnant of that good despite the corruption of the world. This means the disagreement is about just how big that moral remnant is in each of us. It's about just how far we can walk along the moral road by ourselves. It's about the answer to the question: When do the obstacles to love grow too extreme? Where ever the line is drawn, Christianity claims that human power will only go so far, and its nowhere near far enough to pull off Akyol's dream.

Obviously, there is so much more we could bring in to this debate. For now, we simply need to recognize that, plainly, Christians have a very different reason for not following the Muslim Jesus than we identified for Muslims. Muslims think the religious life is unlivable without detailed Law; Christians think it is unlivable under that Law! A choice between competing religious visions is looming here. But before we can properly choose we need to tie up something. I can imagine Muslims thinking: 'Hang on, Christians do claim to follow Jesus! What do you mean by saying that following him is impossible?' Obviously, the apparent inability of Christians to follow Jesus' ethic properly doesn't mean they despair of following him at all. What it does mean is that they see the nature of following Jesus in very different terms from Akyol. To understand this difference, we will need to see just what sort of following the Christian Jesus calls people to.

23

The 'impossible' road of the Christian Jesus

'Follow me!' are the very first words Jesus speaks (to a human) in the Gospel of Matthew:

> As Jesus was walking beside the Sea of Galilee, he saw two brothers, Simon called Peter and his brother Andrew. They were casting a net into the lake, for they were fishermen. 'Come, follow me,' Jesus said, 'and I will send you out to fish for people.' At once they left their nets and followed him. Going on from there, he saw two other brothers, James son of Zebedee and his brother John. They were in a boat with their father Zebedee, preparing their nets. Jesus called them, and immediately they left the boat and their father and followed him. (Matthew 4.18–22)

I've always been struck by this story. As far as we can tell, none of Peter, Andrew, James, or John knew Jesus well. They'd not yet listened to his teaching. They'd not yet witnessed his miracles. Despite this, they dropped everything, abandoned their family and jobs, and followed him. Why? My take is that Matthew wants us to understand, right from the get go, that Jesus, by his presence, words, and actions, powerfully compels devoted following. Even so, if these fishermen had any real sense of just where this road would take them, I wonder if they would have embarked upon it.

At first glance, the path of the Christian Jesus bears deep religious and ethical similarities to the Jesus of Islam. Like the Muslim Jesus, he is walking a Godward road: a road of constant prayer, heavenly focus and holding loosely to worldly blessings. Like the Muslim Jesus, he is walking a virtuous road. It is a road of loving neighbours, speaking truth, visiting the sick, helping the poor, bearing with the annoying, and forgiving the enemy. The extent of Jesus' movement towards those who were not viewed as belonging to God's people was extraordinary. He enjoyed the hospitality of traitors to the Jewish community, drank with the sexually broken, and healed the children of the ruthless oppressors.

The Christian Jesus warned any prospective followers that this sort of ethic is a road less travelled, cautioning them to:

> Enter through the narrow gate. For wide is the gate and broad is the road that leads to destruction, and many enter through it. But small is the gate and narrow the road that leads to life, and only a few find it. (Matthew 7.13–14)

It is also a road that's uncomfortable and unsettling, so he recommended considering the costs involved in walking it:

> When Jesus saw the crowd around him, he gave orders to cross to the other side of the lake. Then a teacher of the law came to him and said, 'Teacher, I will follow you wherever you go.' Jesus replied, 'Foxes have dens and birds have nests, but the Son of Man has no place to lay his head.' Another disciple said to him, 'Lord, first let me go and bury my father.' But Jesus told him, 'Follow me, and let the dead bury their own dead.' (Matthew 8.18–22)

This shocking hyperbole was not to be taken literally – Jesus was not anti-family – but he was deeply God-first. His difficult call was: 'Join me on an unsettled road of uncompromised worship toward God and radical grace toward neighbours of all stripes.'

So yes, the ethics of the Muslim and Christian Jesuses are similar. But – and it's a big 'but' – the following itself is radically different. In fact, at the same time as calling his followers to live out his ethic, Jesus also made it clear that it was not in their power to do so.

An impossible path

The path the Christian Jesus walked placed demands on his original followers that they were, frankly, in no position to fulfil. So, he demanded ethical *perfection*. He said that:

> You have heard that it was said, 'Love your neighbor and hate your enemy.' But I tell you, love your enemies and pray for those who persecute you, that you may be children of your Father in heaven. He causes his sun to rise on the evil and the good and sends rain on the righteous and the unrighteous. If you love those who love you, what reward will you get? Are not even the tax collectors doing that? And if you greet only your own people, what are you doing more than others? Do not even pagans do that? Be perfect, therefore, as your heavenly Father is perfect. (Matthew 5.43–48)

Moral perfection, however, was not enough to follow Jesus. On top of that he expected his followers to do the sorts of miracles he did:

> Truly, truly, I say to you, whoever believes in me will also do the works that I do; and greater works than these will he do ... (John 14.12)

Not only that, he set the requirement for entry into the Kingdom of God as becoming some sort of new person. It wasn't something you could do without an entirely new start at life:

> 'Very truly I tell you, no one can see the kingdom of God unless they are born again.' (John 3.3)

Oh, and there's one more thing. To follow Jesus properly you also need to lose your life:

> And calling the crowd to him with his disciples, he said to them, 'If anyone would come after me, let him deny himself

and take up his cross and follow me. For whoever would save his life would lose it, but whoever loses his life for my sake and the gospel's will save it' (Mark 8.34–35)

We need to feel the force of this. The call to pick up a cross is a call to walk towards a humiliating, painful, loss of self.

So, the sort of following the Christian Jesus has in mind is this: Follow me in being perfect; follow me in walking on water; follow me in casting out demons; follow me in healing the sick; follow me through death; and follow me in becoming a new person. This road appears religiously unreasonable and practically impossible. Jesus, of course, was well aware of this. He knew he was setting an apparently unattainable bar. It took a comparatively mundane discussion about money (what else?) to tease out how he thought it could work.

All things are possible ...

Jesus said this to his disciples:

'How hard it is for the rich to enter the kingdom of God!' The disciples were amazed at his words. But Jesus said again, 'Children, how hard it is to enter the kingdom of God! It is easier for a camel to go through the eye of a needle than for someone who is rich to enter the kingdom of God.' The disciples were even more amazed, and said to each other, 'Who then can be saved?' Jesus looked at them and said, 'With man this is impossible, but not with God; all things are possible with God.' (Mark 10.23–27)

Why were Jesus' disciples amazed by his suggestion that it was difficult for the rich to be God's people? Because they had a religious 'success' mindset. It goes like this: 'People can do what God requires. They can be good, they can be religiously successful, and they can be ethically admirable. This sort of religious success is blessed – indeed rewarded – by God, and a materially and socially successful life is a sign of this divine blessing.' That's how Jesus' hearers thought back then. It's how lots of religious people think today. It is also, incidentally, how lots of Muslims think and Islamic teachers teach.

Everything we've heard from Jesus turns this on its head. He makes it crystal clear that the proper religious road is not humanly possible. Following it successfully is not in our power – it will require the supernatural power of God. The road is not traversed through self-improvement or sustained religious discipline. No. The sort of following that Jesus is talking about involves a profound spiritual, indeed metaphysical transformation. This will require not just God's help, but indeed His personal, empowering, and renewing presence in the life of each follower.

This is precisely what Jesus meant by the idea of being 'born again'. When he first introduced this idea, his hearer asked:

> 'How can a man be born when he is old? Can he enter a second time into his mother's womb and be born?' Jesus answered, 'Truly, truly, I say to you, unless one is born of water and the Spirit, he cannot enter the kingdom of God. That which is born of the flesh is flesh, and that which is born of the Spirit is spirit. Do not marvel that I said to you, "You must be born again." The wind blows where it wishes, and you hear its sound, but you do not know where it comes from or where it goes. So it is with everyone who is born of the Spirit.' (John 3.4–8)

To follow Jesus requires a spiritual rebirth. This is not simply an awakening of interest in spiritual things. That would be just the sort of fleshly – that is human – phenomenon that Jesus is denying suffices. Instead, this is God's Holy Spirit indwelling Jesus' followers and empowering them to live the religious life that they are unable to live by themselves. It is something originating in, and sustained by, God alone.

We must not underestimate the implications of this. It implies that proper, real followers of the Christian Jesus are indwelt by God in a unique, special, transforming way. It also implies that they live lives that are distinctly, radically, supernaturally good. Do we see this in real life? Are Christians noticeably, let alone unquestionably, different? Just how different should we expect them to be? These are all fair questions. We can rightly challenge, examine, test this sort of extraordinary claim. What we cannot do, however, is pretend that the sort of following that the Christian Jesus has in mind here closely – or even distantly – mirrors the sort of following the Muslim Jesus has in *his* mind. This means, of course, that if we are to follow Jesus at all we will need to make a choice between two Jesuses and two types of following. We must decide, in the end, between the two roads.

24

Different roads

My family live on a farm and to visit them I need to leave the sealed highways and travel on rough dirt roads through the bush. Dirt roads and bitumen roads are both roads, of course, but driving on dirt is very different to driving on bitumen. It requires different driving techniques and a different type of vehicle to those suitable for freeways. So, I take a four-wheel drive. Imagine, however, if someone offered to lend me a Ferrari sports car for the weekend to visit the farm. Obviously, it's a brilliant car, and it would be incredibly fun to drive – but only on the bitumen. Once I got to the dirt it would be completely useless. Because it rides so low, on such thin tires and rock-hard suspension, it simply couldn't get over the bumps and rocks involved. In a Ferrari, then, I could get some of the way there, perhaps even most of the way there, in style, but ultimately it couldn't get the job done. To get to the farm I need a four-wheel drive.

Islam and Christianity both describe a road, a path, a way of life. These two roads have some strong similarities. They both describe a God-centred life. They both outline a personal and social ethic that seeks to align with God's good purposes and laws. Importantly, and ultimately, they are both aimed at the same destination: eternal paradise (or heaven). Both claim that Jesus shows us their respective roads and is there to welcome us into eternity (or not!). If I'm right, however, they are very different types of roads, requiring very different religious 'vehicles' to get us to our destination. On the one hand, Islam describes an easy road upon which Muslims can rely on human powered vehicle to take them all the way to a paradise which is the reward for a self-reliant obedient life. On the other, Christianity describes a road that will require a Holy Spirit-powered vehicle to carry the faithful through a range of humanly impossible obstacles to a heaven that is a free gift. How the Muslim and Christian Jesuses negotiated one unique and formidable barrier exhibits this powerfully. That obstacle is the crucifixion.

The road 'towards' and the road 'around'

The Christian Jesus walks a very deliberate road to a death on a cross. Over and again he made it clear that his prime messianic purpose was to head to his crucifixion in Jerusalem to save his people from their sins. He made this explicit the very first time his followers recognized that he was, in fact, the Messiah:

> Now it happened that as he was praying alone, the disciples were with him. And he asked them, 'Who do the crowds say that I am?' And they answered, 'John the Baptist. But others say, Elijah, and others, that one of the prophets of old has risen.' Then he said to them, 'But who do you say that I am?' And Peter answered, 'The Christ [Messiah] of God.' And he strictly charged and commanded them to tell this to no one, saying, 'The Son of Man must suffer many things and be rejected by the elders and chief priests and scribes, and be killed, and on the third day be raised.' (Luke 9.18–22)

This road to the cross, this *via crucis*, is the heart of Christian faith. Jesus calls all his followers to stop trusting their religious selves, and instead, simply rely on the events of the cross for their eternal life:

> And he said to all, 'If anyone would come after me, let him deny himself and take up his cross daily and follow me. For whoever would save his life will lose it, but whoever loses his life for my sake will save it. For what does it profit a man if he gains the whole world and loses or forfeits himself? For whoever is ashamed of me and of my words, of him will the Son of Man be ashamed when he comes in his glory and the glory of the Father and of the holy angels.' (Luke 9.23–27)

For both Jesus and his followers, the road of the cross is paved with shame and loss, but it leads to God's uplifting into eternal glory.

This is no isolated teaching. All four Gospels are built around this narrative. The Gospel of John was once famously described as a crucifixion narrative with an extended introduction, but perhaps the clearest plot summary is found at the end of the Gospel of Luke. There, the resurrected Jesus explains the significance of the cross to his disciples:

> 'These are my words that I spoke to you while I was still with you, that everything written about me in the Law of Moses and the Prophets and the Psalms must be fulfilled.' Then he opened their minds to understand the Scriptures, and said to them, 'Thus it is written, that the Christ should suffer and on the third day rise from the dead, and that repentance for the forgiveness of sins should be proclaimed in his name to all nations, beginning from Jerusalem. You are witnesses of these things.' (Luke 24.44–48)

These few verses don't just summarize Luke's Gospel, they summarize the argument of this book. Everything – *literally everything!* – we've been saying about the Christian Jesus comes together at the cross. The cross is the crowded public event that grounds Christianity in real history, in reliable eyewitness testimony. It is the moment at which all the pieces of the religious puzzle around Jesus fall into place: where the prophecies about the Christ converge; where his salvation names make sense; where the atoning sacrificial divine Law is perfected. It is the precursor to his greatest death-defying miracle: the resurrection. It is the rock upon which Christian self-reliance and pride crumbles, and new identity as redeemed and beloved sinners is grounded. It is the shameful, horrific religious symbol adopted by early Christians to signify the radical, counter-intuitive, even embarrassing disjunction between the road of Jesus and the road of any other religion.

That includes Islam and its Christ.

The Muslim Christ conspicuously avoided the cross. Oh, he was sentenced to be executed upon it, and led there by the crowds, but at the last moment he sidestepped the shame. The Qur'an explains it this way:

> And [for] their saying 'Indeed, we have killed the Messiah, Jesus, the Son of Mary, the messenger of Allah.' And they did not kill him, nor did they crucify him; but [another] was made to resemble him to them. And indeed, those who differ over it are in doubt about it. They have no knowledge of it except the following of assumption. And they did not kill him, for certain. Rather, Allah raised him to Himself ... (Q4.157–158)

Again, the Qur'an seeks to correct Christian doctrine. This time through a clear denial of Jesus' death on the cross.

Ironically (like the Muslim Jesus himself) these self-confident verses are enigmatic – and controversial. The precise understanding of the victim replacement on view here remains disputed in Islamic scholarship. (You can see one obvious problem: how could God kill an innocent third party?) The grounds for the denial of the traditional Christian history are not explained, and neither are the false assumptions that Christians are supposedly laboring under. The grounds for the certainty with which the Qur'an asserts that Jesus survived are left unexplored too. For Muslims, no doubt, it rests in the Islamic logic we identified before: it must be true because the Qur'an is the word of God.

What isn't controversial, of course, is that Islamic teaching has always categorically denied the cross of Christ. It denies the historicity of the event. It denies the atonement theology that explains it. And it denies the sort of religious life that Jesus was calling people to. Islam does so because the Qur'an denies it; because it sees a range of associated philosophical and ethical problems to do with God participating in his creation like that; and because it can't accept that humans need that sort of help. Islam asks: If humans can be religiously successful, then why the cross? Why the need for a Saviour if we don't need saving? Why the offer of spiritual help when we don't need it? Why admit I'm a failure when I'm travelling well?

These reservations are understandable. The events of the Christian cross story are extraordinary enough to warrant close historical scrutiny. The philosophical and ethical conundrums involved in the claim that God can share in our human experience and responsibilities are profound (if not insurmountable). We can, and should, talk more about them. What we cannot, and should not, do is ignore the deep disparity here. The Muslim and Christian Jesuses are walking very different roads: the Christian Jesus walked directly and purposefully to a cross; the Muslim Jesus went out of his way to avoid it.

What this means, of course, is that, at their heart, Islam and Christianity really are different religions. Very different. The Qur'an describes a beautiful religious walk along a road smooth enough to traverse in your own strength. The Gospels portray a humiliating and mysterious journey in which God carries you over steep and insurmountable obstacles by his Spirit. Indeed, Islam is the spiritual Ferrari to Christianity's four-wheel drive.

25
At a crossroads

Muslims and Christians disagree about Jesus. Our authoritative texts say different things about him, our teachers teach different things about him, and we understand him under very different religious frameworks. The two Jesuses are heading in very different directions, and so Christians and Muslims are left at a crossroads. I'm left with two nagging questions about this: 1) If this is so obvious, then why do thoughtful Muslims like Akyol and Khalidi argue, instead, for a common road? And, 2) How should we move forward from here? Which road should we take? Let me take a stab at suggesting some answers.

Denying the crossroads

The motive behind Muslims calling for a common devotion is plain – and noble. It is to cultivate a posture of harmony and accord between two faiths with a patchy record of getting along. I get it, and I love it. It's a deeply worthy aspiration. But while the motive is admirable, the arguments in support of it are patently inadequate if they rest on a falsely imagined commonality. How can apparently honest, intelligent and reflective researchers (like Akyol and Khalidi) ignore this? Here are three possible reasons.

First, perhaps they place greater weight than me on the fact that Christians and Muslims do agree on many fundamentals. As we've recognized, we agree on a monotheistic metaphysic and thus the moral nature of the universe. We also agree on the existence of miracles and prophetic revelation, the eternal nature of humanity and so much more. This is not insignificant. It means we agree on the obligation and urgency to embark upon the journey as well as the destination – even if we disagree on the sort of road we'll need to take.

Second, I'm conscious that Christianity is jammed full of subtle, complex and, at times, apparently paradoxical doctrines. Heck, many Christians struggle to wrap their heads around them! This leads to long, detailed, technical (and often boring) in-house discussions. I can easily sympathize with instances when those of other faiths have a hard time coming to terms with the more obscure aspects of Christian theology. It makes perfect sense to me that Muslims – who are almost never specialists in Christian scholarship – might be at a loss to grasp the obscure subtleties of Christian doctrine. Let's be clear though. Here I'm probably cutting Muslim writers a little too much slack because the centrality of the cross is absolutely *not* obscure in Christianity.

If these first two factors are understandable, a third is more disappointing. There are times, I think, when Muslims (like all of us) fail to step outside their own religious framework in order to evaluate other religions on their own, foreign terms. Not walking in the shoes of another in order to understand them properly is a failure of both imagination and effort. Even if Muslims were correct that Islam is true and Christianity a false distortion of Islam, it is simply not good enough to assume that Christianity and Islam are the same sort of religious path. But that is just what I think is happening in the Jesus discussion. So, Mustafa Akyol makes this assumption. His whole discussion is deeply – and exclusively – Islamic. The fatal flaw in his call for Christians and Muslims to cultivate a shared devotion to Jesus is that it operates entirely under a Muslim conception of religious devotion as mere obedience to Law. Akyol seems oblivious to the possibility that Christianity might conceive of the relationship between God and humans in different terms. He is not alone.

All the Muslim scholars behind the Common Word document make the same assumption. Their call to embrace obedience to a common Law of love seems entirely ignorant of the fact that, for support, they quoted teaching from Jesus that made the point that humans can't obey that law without Jesus' saving work on the cross!

So, they quote 'Blessed are the peacemakers' without acknowledging that this sermon of Jesus profoundly lays out the Christian life in terms not of success, but failure. For Jesus, the mark of God's people is that they recognize their spiritual bankruptcy and cry out at their, and others, profound inability to live well. Even more telling, they separate Jesus' warning against gaining the world yet losing one's soul from his very next words: 'If anyone would come after me, let him deny himself and take up his cross and follow me.' Scholars of religion should know better than to cherry pick evidence out of context. To pluck Jesus ethical teaching from his salvation road to the cross is to misunderstand and misrepresent him. Again, it is taking him on Islamic terms, not his own. That's poor.

These are suggestions. Muslims can decide for themselves if they are valid. In any case, for good motive or bad, solid research or sloppy, Muslims play down the disagreements on Jesus. But here's the thing: I can't see the point. I see little wrong with disagreeing on Jesus – and lots right.

Embracing the crossroads...

I want to conclude this book with a call for Muslims and Christians to embrace healthy and honest disagreement about Jesus. Let me offer three reasons why.

First, merely seeking common ground on Jesus gets us nowhere good – at least from the Christian perspective. Some Muslims might be happy with the approach. That's because the Jesus we come up with by consensus very nearly is the Muslim Jesus. As we saw earlier, Islam brings virtually nothing new to the table concerning Jesus: no new historical details, no new biographical details, and no new insights into the message he taught. Instead, the Muslim Jesus is essentially the Christian Jesus with all the *objectionable* bits taken out. Of course, Muslims are happy to believe in him! From the Christian angle, though, the common Jesus is Jesus with all the *best* bits left out. He's a Jesus devoid of saving and transforming power. So, sure, Christians can agree with nearly everything that Islam believes about Jesus – but accepting *only* those beliefs leaves Christians with a diminished, impoverished, emasculated Christ. The Jesus of shared devotion, then, is one who has been domesticated, tamed by Islam. Why would Christians buy in? In effect it's Muslims saying to Christians: 'Everything we believe is correct; but *you* need to deny your most treasured convictions.' How is that helpful to anyone? How is it respectful to simply tell someone their tested and considered beliefs are unimportant? Where is the intellectual integrity there?

Second, disagreement about Jesus shouldn't matter. At least not in the way that many people think. Mustafa Akyol's idea is that agreement on Jesus helps us get along socially. I reckon that's nonsense. My hunch is that the best way for Christians and Muslims to get along is for them to passionately follow whichever Jesus they believe to be the true one. We've seen that the Muslim Jesus walks a road that embraces a profound and gracious love of neighbour – even if that neighbour is an enemy. Brilliant! With Akyol, I encourage Muslims to wholeheartedly adopt his ethical model the best they can. If this road is all it's cracked up to be it will surely lead to peace. But why should Christians embrace this road? They claim that Jesus doesn't simply offer a grace ethic, but also access to the empowerment of the Holy Spirit to pull it off. This is even better! And there's this too: If Christians are correct that humans can only love enemies with the help of the Holy Spirit, then following the Christian Jesus is the only hope for the woes of our world. If they are wrong, then there is no loss because there is no harm in Christians throwing themselves at God's feet in utter dependency crying out for him to help them love their enemies. At worst, they would be simply joining Muslims in doing their best to be good neighbours. How could different roads here be a bad thing?

Third, limiting a robust and rigorous pursuit of the *true* Jesus – and not just the common one – does no one any favours. Eternity is at stake. Muslims and Christians both expect Jesus to be the one welcoming them into paradise. The only question is: on what terms? Establishing these terms is the ultimate question for humanity, and so no stone should be left unturned in the pursuit of these truths. No scriptural claim should be granted *a priori* authority; no tradition accorded unconfirmed reliability; no in-house theo-logic adopted uncritically. Any Jesus presenting with a gospel will need to withstand the most diligent and thorough examination scholarship – and life – can muster.

Everything we've seen suggests the Muslim Jesus should approach this sort of public scrutiny with modesty not boldness. Unquestionably, he courts controversy. He is historically and theologically fraught. His narrative is supported by, at best, fringe scholarship and poor critiques of Christian tradition. Khalidi, perhaps the greatest expert on the traditions, concedes that 'the Islamic Jesus … might be a fabrication'. Needing, like any prophet, to earn his historical and theological stripes, he fails. However appealing, however impressive, however helpful his sayings have been to Muslim devotion, without a prior commitment to a Muslim religious framework, he does not stand up to rigorous scrutiny. Put simply: I just don't think he's the true Jesus. And if I think that, why on earth would I devote myself to him in any way?

Doubtless many readers will find this dissatisfying. Perhaps you picked up this book hoping that, like Akyol, I might seek to chart a route through ancient, tired old disagreements to a breakthrough in Christian-Muslim discussion and have been disappointed. Maybe you're feeling that I've offered little new to the conversation – that I'm merely rehashing old Christian dismissals of Islam. I have some sympathy if this is the case. While I'd like to think I've drawn on recent scholarship, and offered at least some new and interesting insights, it is fair to say that I essentially align with the trajectory of traditional Christian critiques of Muslim Christology throughout history. The thing is, I think that is inevitable. I think that's where the evidence takes us.

If I'm right about all this, then Muslims and Christians remain at a crossroads. Any hope for Jesus creating a convergence in their paths seems misplaced. We've seen that the two Jesuses are pointing down very different roads: the Muslim Jesus wants to teach you how to be good; the Christian Jesus want to say 'you can't be good' – at least not on your own! The Muslim Jesus wants to you to be a *better* person; the Christian Jesus wants you to be a *whole new* person. The Muslim Jesus wants you to live gazing upon God; the Christian Jesus wants you to welcome God living in you. At this crossroads you are left with a choice: only the true Jesus can get you to your eternal destination.

Epilogue: The real Jesus

In this book, I set out to accept my friends' challenge and meet the Muslim Jesus. I feel like I have met him! I hope I've done him the justice of meeting him on his own, Islamic terms. To the best of my ability I've tried to place him first in his tradition, and only then to offer a scholarly evaluation as well as a religious comparison to the Christian Jesus. My conclusions as a scholar are in the previous pages. Here I offer a few brief, personal reflections as a follower of the Christian Jesus (still).

Perhaps the most striking (and unexpected) reaction I have is this: the Muslim Jesus I met in the Islamic texts looks a lot like the Sunday School Jesus I had encountered as a child! He is, predominantly, the Christmas and resurrection Jesus. His birth and ascension to heaven are cool. His few miracles are amazing, but safe and un-confronting. He says little and what he does say tends to affirm that I'm religiously OK. As well, he is largely G-rated. Aside from some obscure scary stuff on the judgement day, his life contains no gruesome crucifixions and no intimidating theological paradoxes. He is extraordinary, but not in any way that impacts directly upon my life. Having once 'followed' a Jesus like that, I can see his appeal.

I can't follow him though. That's because, compared to the Christian Jesus I met at university, he just doesn't seem real. Unlike the Jesus of the Bible, he doesn't seem to have lived a real life. Unlike the Jesus I met in the Gospels, his words don't resonate with my real experience of being human. Unlike the Christian Jesus, I have never felt the supernatural power of his spirit flowing through me performing miracles of healing and transformation.

In the end, for me, the Muslim Jesus is good, but imagined, while the Christian Jesus is fantastically and overwhelmingly real. I'm sticking with him.

Select bibliography

On the Muslim Jesus:

Tarif Khalidi, *The Muslim Jesus: Sayings and Stories in Islamic Literature*, Harvard University Press: Cambridge, 2001.

Mustafa Akyol, *The Islamic Jesus: How the king of the Jews became a prophet of the Muslims*, St Martins: New York, 2017.

On the historical Jesus:

Martin Hengel, *The Four Gospels and the One Gospel of the Lord Jesus Christ*, Trinity Press: Harrisburg, 2000.

Richard Bauckham, *Jesus and the Eyewitnesses: The Gospels as Eyewitness Testimony*, Eerdmans: Grand Rapids, 2006.

John Dickson, *The Christ Files*, Blue Bottle: Sydney, 2006.

Paul Barnett, *Is the New Testament History*, Aquila Press: Sydney, 1987.

On the religious Jesus:

Robert M. Bowman Jr. and J. Ed Komoszewski, *Putting Jesus in His Place: The Case for the Deity of Christ*, Kregel: Grand Rapids, 2007.

Michael F. Bird ed., *How God Became Jesus*, Zondervan: Grand Rapids, 2014.

Endnotes

1   Khalidi, T., *The Muslim Jesus: Sayings and Stories in Islamic Literature*,
    Harvard University Press: Cambridge, 2001, p.6.
2   Watt, W.M., *Muhammad at Mecca*, Clarendon: Oxford, 1953, p.27.
3   Ibn Ishaq, *The Life of Muhammad* (Translation Alfred Guillaume),
    Oxford University Press: Oxford, p.271.
4   Khalidi, p.14.
5   Khalidi, p.12.
6   Sahih al-Bukhari 3438.
7   Sahih al-Bukhari 3395, 3396, Sahih Muslim 165 a, Sahih Muslim 165
    b, Sahih al-Bukhari 3239, Sahih al-Bukhari 3394, Sahih Muslim 167.
8   Sahih Muslim Book 19, Hadith 1.
9   Ibn Ishaq, p.653.
10 Al-Tabari, *The History of Al-Tabari*, Vol IV, SUNY: New York, 1987, p. 124f.
11 Al-Tabari records this fulfilling a prophecy of Isaiah, Matthew
    records it fulfilling Hosea 11.1.
12 Al-Tabari, p.121.
13 Khalidi, p.26.
14 Khalidi, p.29.
15 Khalidi, p.130.
16 Khalidi, p.52.
17 Khalidi, p.126.
18 Khalidi, p.76.
19 Khalidi, p.71.
20 Khalidi, p.138.
21 Khalidi, p.152.
22 Khalidi, p.187.
23 Khalidi, p.201.
24 Khalidi, p.206.
25 Khalidi, p.41.
26 Khalidi, p.29f.
27 Khalidi, p.19.

28 Akyol, p.35.
29 Akyol, p.7f.
30 Akyol, p.80.
31 Akyol, p.151.
32 Akyol, p.204.
33 <http://edition.cnn.com/2006/BUSINESS/08/17/tobacco.ruling/>
34 Akyol, p.2f.
35 Akyol, p.74.
36 Barnett, P., *Is the New Testament History*, Aquila: Sydney, 1986.
37 Muhammad 'Ata ur-Rahim, *Jesus A Prophet of Islam*, Tahrike Tarsile Qur'an, 1996 p.39f.
38 Akyol, p.82.
39 Oddbjorn Leirvik, *Images of Jesus Christ in Islam*, Bloomsbury: London, 2010, p.114.
40 Akyol, p.36.
41 Akyol, p.37.
42 Akyol, p.37.
43 Akyol, p.41.
44 Akyol, p.39.
45 Akyol, p.56.
46 Akyol, p.103.
47 <http://www.newadvent.org/fathers/0103126.htm>
48 <https://www.ccel.org/ccel/schaff/npnf201.iii.viii.xxvii.html>
49 <http://www.newadvent.org/fathers/2708.htm>
50 Origen, *The Fathers of the Church: Origen, Commentary on the Gospel of John, Books 1–10*, Catholic University of America Press: Washington, 1989, p.116.
51 Griffith, S.H., *The Bible in Arabic: The Scriptures of the 'People of the Book' in the Language of Islam*, Princeton University Press: New Jersey, 2015, p.47.
52 Khalidi, p.14.
53 Bannister, A., *An Oral-Formulaic Study of the Qur'an*, Lexington: Lanham, 2014.
54 Khalidi, p.17.
55 Shumack, R., *The Wisdom of Islam and the Foolishness of Christianity*, Island View: Sydney, 2015.

56 For example, Moses, Elijah and Daniel were Jewish prophets accompanied by dramatic miracles – although with nothing like the regularity or centrality of Jesus' miracles.

57 Al-Tabari, p.121.

58 Ismael al-Faruqi, *Islam*, Niles: Argus, 1979, p.9.

59 Robert Bowman, J. Komoszewski, Putting Jesus in His Place: The Case for the Deity of Christ, Kregel: Grand Rapids, 2007, pp.265-268 (Kindle Edition).

60 Akyol, p.216.

61 Khalidi, p.43.

62 Khalidi, p.202.

63 Akyol, pp.202-203.

64 Akhtar, S., *A Faith for All Seasons: Islam and Western Modernity*, Ivan R. Dee: Chicago, 1990, p.160.

65 Akhtar, S., *The Qur'an and the Secular Mind: A Philosophy of Islam*, Routledge: Abingdon, 2008, p.277.

66 Khalidi, p.45.

WE HAVE A VISION OF A WORLD IN WHICH EVERYONE IS TRANSFORMED BY CHRISTIAN KNOWLEDGE

As well as being an award-winning publisher, SPCK is the oldest Anglican mission agency in the world.

Our mission is to lead the way in creating books and resources that help everyone to make sense of faith.

Will you partner with us to put good books into the hands of prisoners, great assemblies in front of schoolchildren and reach out to people who have not yet been transformed by the Christian faith?

To donate, please visit www.spckpublishing.co.uk/donate or call our friendly fundraising team on 020 7592 3900.